Financial Analysis and Business Decisions on the Pocket Calculator
Jon M. Smith

Managing Innovation
Edwin A. Gee and Chaplin Tyler

The Management System: Systems Are for People
Leslie H. Matthies

Financial Accounting Estimates through Statistical Sampling by Computer
Maurice S. Newman

Forecasting Methods for Management, Second Edition
Steven C. Wheelwright and Spyros Makridakis

Decision Making and Planning for the Corporate Treasurer
Harold Bierman, Jr.

Corporate Financial Planning Models
Henry I. Meyer

Strategies in Business
Shea Smith, III, and John E. Walsh, Jr.

Program-Management Control Systems
Joseph A. Maciariello

Contemporary Cash Management: Principles, Practices, Perspective
Paul J. Beehler

Dynamic Cost Reduction
Irving Dlugatch

Dynamic
Cost Reduction

Dynamic
Cost Reduction

IRVING DLUGATCH

California Western University

A Ronald Press Publication

JOHN WILEY & SONS, New York · Chichester · Brisbane · Toronto

Library of Congress Cataloging in Publication Data

Dlugatch, Irving, 1910-
  Dynamic cost reduction.

  (Systems and controls for financial management series)
  "A Ronald Press publication."
  Includes index.
  1. Cost control.   I. Title.   II. Series.
HD47.5.D58   658.1'552   78-21078
ISBN 0-471-03565-3

Printed in the United States of America

10 9 8 7 6 5 4 3 2 1

To Helen

SERIES PREFACE

No one needs to tell the reader that the world is changing. He sees it all too clearly. The immutable, the constant, the unchanging of a decade or two ago no longer represent the latest thinking—on *any* subject, whether morals, medicine, politics, economics, or religion. Change has always been with us, but the pace has been accelerating, especially in the postwar years.

Business, particularly with the advent of the electronic computer some 20 years ago, has also undergone change. New disciplines have sprung up. New professions are born. New skills are in demand. And the need is ever greater to blend the new skills with those of the older professions to meet the demands of modern business.

The accounting and financial functions certainly are no exception. The constancy of change is as pervasive in these fields as it is in any other. Industry is moving toward an integration of many of the information gathering, processing, and analyzing functions under the impetus of the so-called systems approach. Such corporate territory has been, traditionally, the responsibility of the accountant and the financial man. It still is, to a large extent—but times are changing.

Does this, then, spell the early demise of the accountant as we know him today? Does it augur a lessening of influence for the financial specialists in today's corporate hierarchy? We think not. We maintain, however, that it is incumbent upon today's accountant and today's financial man to learn *today's* thinking and to *use today's* skills. It is for this reason the Systems and Controls for Financial Management Series is being developed.

Recognizing the broad spectrum of interests and activities that the series title encompasses, we plan a number of volumes, each representing the latest thinking, written by a recognized authority, on a particular facet of the financial man's responsibilities. The subjects contemplated for discussion within the series range from production accounting systems to planning, to corporate records, to control of cash. Each book is an in-depth study of one subject within this group. Each is intended to be a practical, working tool for the businessman in general and the financial man and accountant in particular.

ROBERT L. SHULTIS
FRANK M. MASTROMANO

PREFACE

An accepted management theory is that the primary function of management is producing a profit. Any business organization must be profitable to justify its existence. Even nonprofit organizations must show a profit. The bottom line is the significant line for assessing the health of the organization.

The present state-of-the-art in management stresses productivity as the key to improved profits. The theory is that increased production at lower unit cost means higher profits. This theory holds that cost control is of utmost importance. Cost control needs goals and plans—operating budgets or cost standards. Cost control is concerned with keeping unit costs below established standards under existing conditions.

As long as the cost standards are not exceeded, management believes that its cost control is effective. When the competition starts to undersell and remains profitable, it is time to re-examine the cost standards.

It is time for cost reduction.

Such one-shot campaigns might properly be called *Static Cost Reduction*. The effect on the profit, if any, is not readily determined until some time has elapsed.

The purpose of this book is to introduce a new approach, *Dynamic Cost Reduction*. It is a method for setting *readily achievable* cost standards for every phase of company operations, not just for production. Criteria for the cost standards are the impact they have on the *desired* profit in a competitive market. Dynamic Cost Reduction deals with the present environment, not with company operations in the past.

It is dynamic, because it is a continuing function. Cost standards can be adjusted in immediate response to a change in the market. These adjustments can be made at any time, without traumatic cuts or expensive investments. Industrial engineering deals with men and machines. DCR deals with dollars and profits.

Static cost reduction is based on the productivity concept, but Dynamic Cost Reduction stems from the profitability concept.

The development of DCR was caused by an increasing concern I found among clients over the inadequacies of industrial engineering for profit improvement. It was first necessary to examine the productivity approach for its weaknesses and its strengths. I found many large companies were already applying the profitability concept but with no large improvement, because the only tool available was static cost reduction. DCR is the technique that makes the profitability concept effective.

The book introduces the concept of DCR—what it is, how it works, and what it can do. It is an expansion of the presentations that have been made to company managements for the purpose of explaining DCR and the benefits to be derived from its use. The maximum realization of these benefits is attained when the program is developed and implemented by management and staff with minimum assistance from outside consultants. This is important to ensure that the improvements under DCR will be continued beyond the organizational and planning stages.

This is intended to be a management textbook and not a mathematical treatise. Although mathematics can not be avoided, throughout the stress is on interpreting the data rather than on how the data was obtained. Toward that end, no derivations or in-depth discussions of mathematical or, for that matter, management theory are included. Computational exercises are essential to the understanding of the tools used. These are reduced, in all cases, to simple formulas.

The effectiveness of the cost reduction program depends quite heavily on good cost controls. Too often reliance is placed on historical data and probabilistic estimates. Techniques are described for achieving better controls. Chief among these are some new applications of short interval scheduling. Because short interval scheduling is not widely used today (perhaps because it has been misapplied in the past) considerable space is allotted to it, including much that has never appeared in print.

The plan of this book is to lead the reader through the basic concepts of management concerned with profitability. Current practice is to compute profit as the difference between the selling price and the cost of sales. This leads to an emphasis on productivity, the control of unit cost. Cost standards under the productivity concept are usually based on historical data. When cost reductions are needed, the production costs are attacked, because managers are most familiar with this area and productivity is highly visible. The impact on the profit is not readily determined until some time after the cost reductions have been implemented.

Cost standards for the Dynamic Cost Reduction method are tied to the market and the desired profit. Subtracting the *goal profit* from the selling price gives the *goal cost of sales*. Achievable cost standards are defined for, not the factory alone, but every phase of company operations including the cost of money. The impact on the profit is known immediately.

It is important to the success of DCR that the managerial resources of the company be properly organized into a planning task force. Toward this end, one chapter is devoted to such organization and the techniques that are needed for effective planning. Additional material in other chapters deals with control methods that ar necessary to ensure the continued effectiveness of the program. An important asset of DCR is that only minor changes are needed in reporting procedures and in management information systems. Thus the cost of implementing DCR is considerably lower than that of a conventional industrial engineering program.

Static Cost Reduction depends heavily on sales volume for its success. High volume does not necessarily mean high profits. Dynamic Cost Reduction is independent of sales volume and is tied to the profit needed for growth. Thus, SCR is like paying commissions on sales of low profit but easy-to-sell products; DCR is like paying commissions only on sales that yield a substantial profit.

Irving Dlugatch

Los Angeles, California
January 1979

CONTENTS

Dynamic
Cost Reduction

CHAPTER 1

THE PRODUCTIVITY CONCEPT

The basis for modern management is the productivity concept. It is believed that profits are directly related to the productivity, that high efficiency means low costs and therefore maximum profits. A number of fallacies in this theory will be discussed in this chapter.

The foundation was laid for modern scientific management by Adam Smith in the eighteenth century. He was the first to suggest that productivity was a measure of industry's effectiveness, and, that by adding or improving machines or by better use of the labor force, productivity would increase. Frederick W. Taylor, in developing his principles of management, placed emphasis on shop management. He was concerned with efficiency in the factory, using time and motion studies. (6)

INDUSTRIAL ENGINEERING

Industrial engineering is the modern technology that has evolved from the early work of the "efficiency" experts. Industrial engineering is still generally confined to production activities and those areas that interface with the factory. It is difficult to convince managers that Taylor's basic principles are applicable to all aspects of their business. This is understandable, since industrial engineers describe themselves as being concerned with the design, improvement, and installation of integrated systems of men, materials, and equipment. (8)

Management feels that the management function is a nontechnical activity and production is a technical one. This has led to a great deal of specialization among industrial engineers, not only in industries, but also in branches of industry. Only recently the meat packing industry opened its doors to industrial engineers. Meat packers couldn't believe that tool and die people would understand sausages. Foundry people will not talk with anyone who hasn't worked in a foundry.

PRODUCTIVITY

It is a common belief that management is an art and therefore cannot have measures of productivity. The same reasoning is applied to other areas of the business, such as research, design, purchasing, marketing, and finance.

But productivity is a common consideration in all these areas. To be productive is to yield results, benefits, or profits. Productivity is the quality of being productive. Note that productivity is not necessarily synonymous with profit. What we shall call the *productivity concept* of management is an abstraction of the Taylor principles. Consider Figure 1. The figure is a model of a firm under the productivity concept. Management science and management experience offers little in the way of tools for increasing profits in any area except production.

The propaganda of the industrial engineers has convinced most manufacturers that profit is directly related to productivity. The theory is that, if the number of units manufactured is increased 10% while the unit cost goes up only 5%, there will be a substantial profit increase.

For example, a consumer products manufacturer installed a preven-

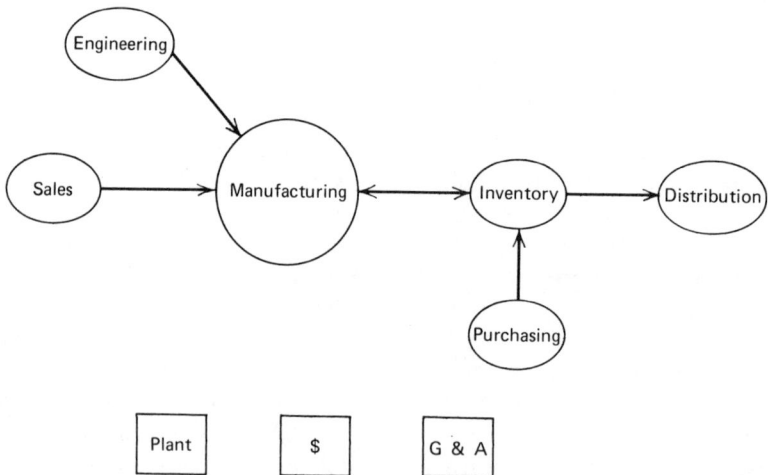

Figure 1   Productivity Concept Model of the Firm

tive maintenance program and replaced a number of materials handlers with a conveyor. These improvements reduced the unit cost. An incentive pay system offset the cost reductions but was responsible for an increase in production. Net reduction in unit costs was 20%, but the pretax profit margin was reported as increasing from 8% to 21%. These figures are probably correct because the company had lost its share of the market due to soaring labor costs. The cost reductions permitted the company to compete again. (8)

Analyzing this case, we see a prime example of the productivity concept at work. The production costs loom large in the eyes of management. They know that the competition is selling identical products at a lower price. Therefore, the competition must surely have a more efficient factory.

Questions that suggest themselves are:

1. Was the competition truly more efficient?
2. Was the profit improvement temporary or permanent?
3. If the problem reoccurs in the future, can industrial engineering help?

These questions go to the heart of the problem with the productivity concept. Cost reduction under this concept is static, a solution for an immediate problem. Industrial engineers categorize productivity as an activity that maximizes the input factors into the industrial enterprise of materials, labor, facilities, and administration. Implicit in this definition is the assumption that the productivity solution is the optimum solution. Therefore, they feel it is *the* solution. In the pages that follow, it will be demonstrated that there are other solutions to the problem of low or no profits.

EXPERIENCE CURVES (1, 2, 3, 4, 5)

The productivity concept is responsible for an important management planning tool, the experience or learning curve. The idea behind these curves is that experience improves performance. Part of the theory is that the company that has produced the largest quantity will be the most efficient. The learning curve was developed by the Air Force. In its most common form, a learning curve relates the labor hours required to perform a task with the number of times the task has been performed. For a large number of activities, the learning curve takes the form of Figure 2.

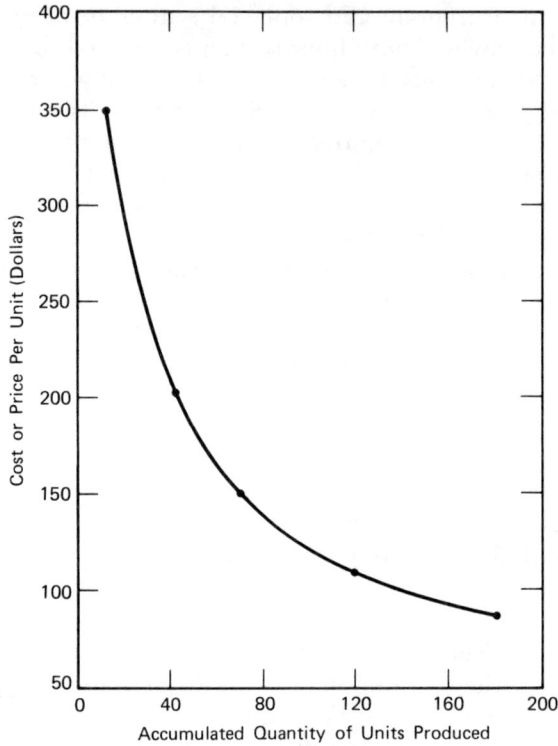

Figure 2   Learning Curve

The time to perform an activity decreases by a constant percentage whenever the number of trials is doubled. The individual worker as well as the assembly line as a unit becomes more efficient with experience. Since learning increases the efficiency of an operation, it should reduce the cost of that operation. Therefore, Figure 2 relates dollars with volume instead of time with output. A 20% reduction in hours for each doubling of performances (called an 80% curve) is typical of a wide variety of tasks. For Figure 2, the cost goes down from $200 to $140 when the accumulated volume doubles from 40 to 80. This is a 30% reduction in costs, and the curve is a 70% curve.

Slopes sharper than 80% (about 70–75%) represent faster learning than normal. This can occur only with the application of new technology or partial mechanization, reducing the time needed to perform the activity.

Figure 2 implies that improvement continues forever. This is because the base of the curve is not time but trials. The number of trials required for a given percent improvement grows enormously as learning occurs. As a result, learning appears static.

Sometimes two products may have learning curves with different slopes, although they are made in the same factory and are similar products. This does not mean that the industrial engineers are derelict. The sharper slope is probably due to special technology or automation. One can be certain that if the poorer curve could be improved, the company would most certainly do so.

If cost declines predictably with units produced, the company producing the most units should have the lowest cost. Assuming all competitors sell at the same price, the competitor with the most unit experience should enjoy the greatest profit. Furthermore, very substantial differences in cost and profit should exist between competitors having widely different unit experiences. It is assumed that all competitors are equally efficient and have equal resources and patents.

The costs have a very strong relationship to the company's share of the competitive market. Over a period of time when market positions are relatively stable, experience can also be equated with market share. Figure 3 represents a stable market (which occurs only after a reasonable period of time) and shows a typical relationship in market shares. Note the similarity to Figure 2.

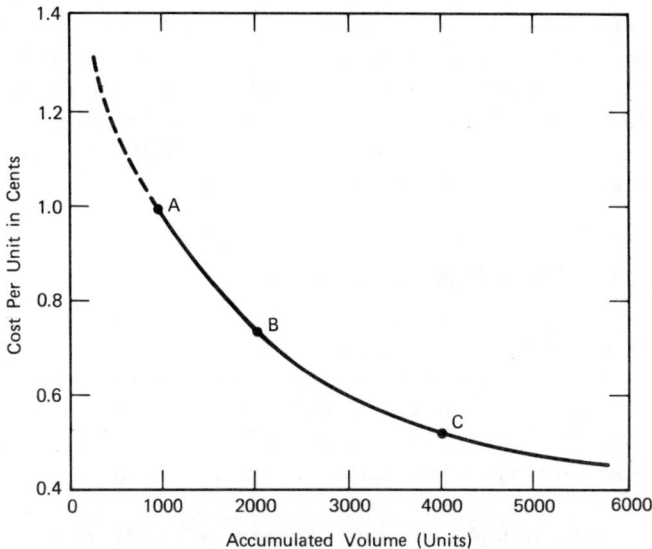

Figure 3   Market Share and Costs for Three Competitors

Observe that Competitor C dominates the market with about 50% of the market. If the market is growing 15% or more annually in units, then the dominant producer may have much more than 50% of the market, because he will have a major portion of the increase.

In any case, an important point is that A and B have little chance of overtaking C in market share, even if they eventually achieve the same unit cost as C. The positions of A and B on the curve indicate that they either had poor learning curve slopes or came into the market late. By the time A and B achieve the same efficiency as C on the present chart, C will have lowered its unit cost further. Even if the reduction is slight, C will still maintain an edge. By the same reasoning, A cannot overtake B. Of course, there will be minor changes in the market shares.

Any attempt at unit cost reduction for the purpose of capturing a larger share of the market (higher productivity) is wasted effort. Larger market shares can be attained by product improvement and innovative marketing campaigns.

One example of this is found in the instant photography industry. Polaroid and Kodak have very similar systems and prices. It is highly unlikely that Kodak will ever capture a major share of this market. Polaroid is too solidly entrenched and is spending a great deal of money on research and development in order to stay on top.

The implications of experience curves are large. They were probably a factor in the decisions made by the consumer goods manufacturer in our first example. That firm apparently determined the value of an increase in market share in terms of improved cost and increased volume. The investment required to increase the share in the market can be compared with that calculated value. In this case, the investment was very low, a relatively small fee to the industrial engineering consultant and the cost of purchasing a conveyor.

PRODUCTIVITY MEASUREMENT (7)

Productivity is theoretically output divided by labor. In practice, this measure is difficult to apply. Output's value varies with price and quality, and there are different kinds of output. For example, there is dollar value, physical volume, value added, or capital investment. In the chemical industry, for instance, few companies use the same measure.

The chemical industry, like many others, generally defines productivity as output per employee, and retail businesses often divide their

dollar volume by the number of salespeople. Those using such a measure believe worker efficiency is directly proportional to this ratio. Of
course, its value is only in comparison with past productivity and does
not really measure efficiency or unit costs.

The Enjay Chemical Company divides the total number of employees into the dollar sales volume, less materials and energy costs. Dow
Chemical determines its manpower utilization yield by dividing its
gross profit before overhead deductions by the cost of manpower. The
Celanese method is to subtract materials and energy costs from sales
revenue to obtain value added. The value added is then divided by the
number of employees to get a measure of productivity.

The chief reason for this lack of uniformity is that no one has found a
way of measuring the effect of all the resources of a company on its
productivity. How is maintenance productivity measured? What is the
contribution of capital to increased productivity?

John W. Kendrick of George Washington University developed a
measure called *Total Factor Productivity* that takes into account contributions by both labor and capital. He uses two partial indices. His
first defines labor productivity in the usual way by relating output to
labor alone.

Capital productivity, Mr. Kendrick's second index, relates the increase in productivity to capital alone. Capital includes land, plant,
equipment, and inventory.

The two indices are weighted according to the relative returns on
capital and payments to labor and then combined into a single index.
The chief criticism of the Kendrick index has been that it combines
two unlike quantities.

A more widely used measure is *partial productivity,* the ratio of
physical output to a single input, usually labor. Whenever productivity is discussed, *labor productivity* is implied, the real output per hour
of work. One reason for its common use is that it seems to be readily
measured.

In reality, productivity measurement is not a simple matter. There
are too many non-quantifiable factors involved. Service industries are
particularly difficult, because there is no physical output to be measured. Also, in all industries, the effect of anti-pollution and OSHA
costs cannot be computed.

There are two ways to measure productivity—comparison with past
performance or industry levels, and engineered standards. Engineered work standards are developed by time and motion studies
and are essentially the optimum productivity that can be achieved by
the *average* worker for a specific station. Productivity is then some

percentage of the engineered standard (70% is poor; 90%, good). Historical data is used for comparison purposes and is based on the productivity achieved in the past by the *average* worker. Productivity is again some percentage of the historical work standard.

A whole new technology has developed called *human engineering*. Its objective is to design machines that can be most efficiently operated by men. The "average" man is of some concern to designers in his new field. They have found that individuals differ in such things as reaction time, strength of grip, and visual acuity. Also, an individual differs from time to time in the same characteristic. Thus, it becomes evident that both engineered and historical standards need to be constantly updated as the workforce changes.

Both measures are of value in measuring the productivity of a company and in making decisions on changes. Engineered standards are available for many industries. These can be compared with a company's current standards and the advisability of changes can be determined.

Should the efficiency prove to be below that of the industry there are several possible causes:

1. Employee morale.
2. Machines are less efficient than those used by other companies.
3. Machines are improperly used or maintained.
4. Problems with materiel or logistics.
5. Poor production controls.

Any good industrial engineer can quickly correct these problems. Whether the corrections will restore the competitiveness is another question. The learning curve is responsible for the belief that competitiveness is a function of productivity.

The heavy reliance on historical data both for the company and the industry suggests a need for a clearer understanding and evaluation of what constitutes past performance. There is limited capability in most organizations to identify and isolate the trends in productivity, both in-house and in-industry, which have an impact on profitability.

Example: The Good Life Company, producing vitamins and health foods, found itself losing its dominant position in the market. The company had an excellent industrial engineering staff that was continuously monitoring the factory efficiency and introducing automation.

It was decided to compare the company's plants with industry

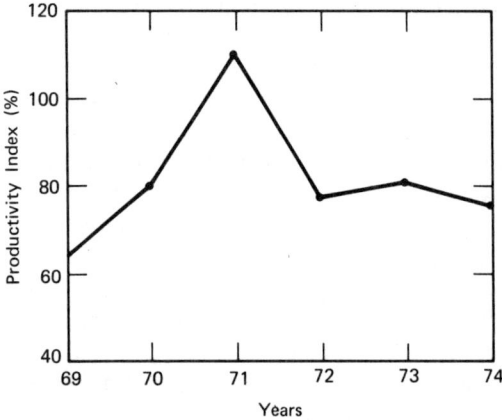

Figure 4   Productivity Trends for Good Life Co.

averages. The only available data was the Productivity Index published by the Federal Bureau of Labor Statistics. The Index is the output per total employee manhours. The Productivity Index showed an average annual gain of 2% for the 5-year period, 1969–74. Good Life found its average annual gain for the same period was only 1.2%. Recognizing that simple averages mask the true trend, the industrial engineers plotted a set of curves for the period as shown in Figure 4.

Examination of the curve showed dramatically that, in truth, the company's productivity was falling instead of rising. The only real increase had occurred in 1971, one year after the installation of automatic production machinery. This was followed by a 30% drop in the productivity from which the factory never recovered.

Such data could well trigger an expensive factory cost reduction program. Unfortunately such a program would fail to alleviate the situation. A similar plot for each of the individual companies in the industry might have shown essentially the same trends. This is true for most industries.

If Good Life was losing its dominance of the market, it was not likely that the problem was in its productivity, at least for its factory. It might have been more rewarding to explore its marketing and distribution areas for the causes.

PROBABILISTIC FACTORS

Industrial engineers may set up performance standards promising very high productivity. But the promise may never be fulfilled because of factors over which the manager has no control. Most managerial estimates and forecasts are based on probabilistic data. Most managerial decisions are similarly derived. Since all planning is for future activities and the future is uncertain, the manager must rely on probability theory. A useful approach is to treat uncertainty in terms of risk. Risk requires the gathering of additional information, insights, judgments, experiences, hunches, and intuitions to be able to make a sound probability estimate. Probability estimates frequently require both objective and subjective probabilities.

Probabilities are objective if nearly everybody would arrive at the same values. Probabilities are subjective if they are determined by judgment, intuition, and experience.

The extent to which the productivity concept relies on probability theory is best illustrated by an example.

Example: The Cowan Company is about to penetrate the market for digital watches with an expensive ladies model. Two items are needed—estimate of demand, and quantities to be manufactured for maximum profit. The demand estimate is obtained by statistical analysis of samplings of the markets. Such analyses are very likely to arrive at several different estimates each with its own probability. Obviously the unit costs will vary with the quantity of units produced. The market research organization provided Cowan with the data in Table 1.1.

The Cowan production manager computed the profits to be expected for the three alternatives. (Note that the probabilities add up to unity.) This is because the three alternatives are the only possibilities. Only one can occur but most certainly one of them will be selected. The table is now expanded to that of Table 1.2.

The range of profit is very large with an average of $450,000. The average is not the best indicator, since it implies that each of

TABLE 1.1 COWAN COMPANY MARKET RESEARCH DATA

Market (Units)	Probability
10,000	.25
20,000	.25
40,000	.50

TABLE 1.2   EXPANDED MARKET DATA

Market (Units)	Probability	Returns
10,000	.25	$-400,000
20,000	.25	200,000
40,000	.50	1,500,000

the possible markets is equally likely. In addition, the manager is likely to have some intuitive feeling about the most probable outcome, despite any advice to the contrary from his staff or consultants. This will be reflected in his evaluation of each of the outcomes. He will select his own probabilities for the outcomes and use them to calculate new values of returns. The calculation consists of multiplying the estimated return by the probability of the market. The result of the computation is the expectation of the particular alternative. It is also called the *weighted return* and is the manager's biased conclusion. The final table is in the form of Table 1.3.

The primary interest in the possible success of undertaking the new product is indicated by the average expectation. The average shows a favorable outcome for attempting the product. A negative value or a very low positive value would indicate the program will be a failure.

There still remains considerable uncertainty. For example,

1. There is some minimum return below which it might be more profitable to invest in a different program.
2. A return of $1,500,000 is attractive, but the risk may be higher than the manager would care to take. He can look just as good bringing in $30,000 on a low-risk project.
3. A loss of $40,000 is more damaging for the manager in the eyes of top management than a gain of $1,500,000 is beneficial.

TABLE 1.3   FINALIZED MARKET DATA

Market (Units)	Probability	Returns	Weighted Returns
10,000	.25	$-400,000	$-100,000
20,000	.25	200,000	50,000
40,000	.50	1,500,000	750,000
	Average	$ 450,000	$ 233,333

These three items are an evaluation of the manager's value system. He can organize his goals as a manager and his assessment of the relative importance of gains and risks into something called a *utility function*. (9, 10)

The utility function can be used to calculate new expectations. Surprisingly this computation gives an average expectation of −2. This indicates the project should not be initiated because of extremely high risk. This is in violent contrast to the first intuitive estimates. Such disparate results from different approaches are always to be expected from probabilistic techniques. There is always some doubt about which answer is the correct one.

The manager's decisions are based heavily on profit estimates which, in turn, depend on the unit cost. It is for that reason that he needs the industrial engineer to ensure the lowest unit cost. The industrial engineer, however, is not in the least interested in sales volume or profits. He has a very narrow viewpoint, the direct labor cost of specific manufacturing operations.

PRODUCTIVITY AND PROFIT

The early works of Taylor and Fayol were concerned with productivity without concern for profits. Only the brashest of industrial engineers would make claims about the amount of profit improvement gained with each percent of productivity increase.

A study of industrial engineering clients by E. C. Baum and Associates of Chicago found that 4–6% of the annual direct payroll was needed for the industrial engineering budget. Without this support, the unit cost could deteriorate about 5% in one year. Improvements claimed by most industrial engineers are in the order of 15–35%. Thus, maintenance of improvement can cost between one–eighth and one–third of savings. (8)

Industrial engineering consultant fees can run as high as 10% of the annual direct payroll. For a 5-year period (a common planning period), the consultant services could take 2% of the savings.

In the example given early in this chapter, a 20% saving was realized by the installation of a preventive maintenance program and a conveyor. The conveyor cost can be amortized over a long period and so does not contribute substantially to the cost of the improvements. The cost of the maintenance program depends on the number of inspections per year, the number of men needed for the program, and the cost of the down-time required for the inspections. Add to this the cost of failures that are not prevented by the inspections. The program costs must be substantially less than the cost of the down-time without preventive maintenance. Involved in this calculation are the probabilities of the failures. Few industrial engineers are familiar with the mathematics for obtaining an optimum preventive maintenance program. Yet many of them persist in selling such programs to naive managements.

The reduction in the number of material handlers because of the installation of a conveyor is not without some cost. Even if jobs can be found elsewhere in the company for the excess personnel, there are still the costs of processing and retraining. If part of work force must be terminated, there are termination costs, not the least of which is the penalty the company must pay in higher State taxes.

All of these cost items tend to cast doubt on claims of substantial profit gains from even small increases in productivity. One can readily arrive at the conclusion that profit improvement by raising productivity is a risky business.

Many production problems exist, even in relatively small operations, for which the solutions are obscured by complexity. As an example, a production line may be used for a number of models of a product. The capacity of the line is known, but the orders for various models vary randomly. In order to keep the line running at capacity (for lowest unit cost) it is necessary to develop an optimum production schedule. Queuing theory, which can deal with fluctuations on a production line, is useful for this purpose. A queuing theory analysis may well determine that the productivity is not limited by worker efficiency but by machine capacity or by lead times.

There is an important question that must be asked. Does lower unit cost arise from increased volume with no increase in costs or no increase in volume but decreased costs? In the first case, the increased volume means increased inventory costs plus increased marketing and distribution costs. In the second case, higher profits can be realized only by using the last-in-first-out inventory technique. The old units in inventory must eventually be sold at a loss.

INCREASING PRODUCTIVITY

Our concern with productivity is with its affects on profits. We need to examine the common techniques employed for increasing productivity to determine how best to use them to improve profits.

It is a common practice to increase the work force to permit meeting current and near-future demands for a company's products. When demand falls off, layoffs are initiated. If we plot such a cycle (in terms of labor cost dollars) over a period of years, we might obtain a projection such as the solid line of Figure 5.

Note that the range of labor cost is very wide. Employees are well aware of the feast-or-famine cycle of jobs. With layoffs always imminent, regardless of seniority, morale is never very high in this kind of company. Add to this that people work in hourly jobs in factories, even when not members of a union. They will usually perform only at the level and output which will keep them from dismissal. In such a situation the standard hour is not likely to be one that will yield maximum profits, and, any attempt to increase productivity based on engineered changes in the standard hours, is not likely to be successful. There is no incentive for the work force to increase its productivity, because employees see only an effective wage cut and a probable hastening of layoffs as inventory builds up. Incentive payments do not increase productivity. They merely increase the output without change in the cost of production.

Observe the dotted line in Figure 5. This is a plot of productivity, and though it fluctuates considerably more than the total payroll dollars, the actual fluctuation is only a few percent.

The fluctuation can be less than plus or minus 5%, despite such plus and minus factors as wage increases, price competition, material cost increases, turnover and absenteeism, quality problems, improved methods, new machines, price increases, design improvements, and new products.

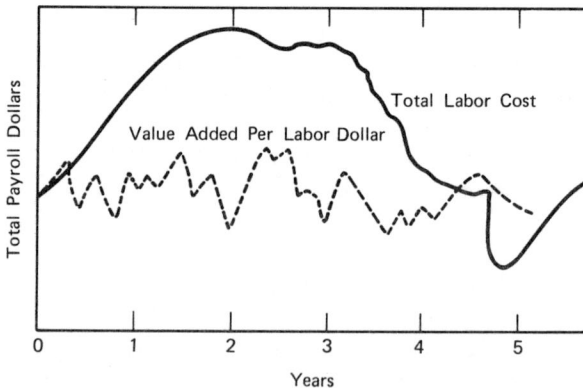

Figure 5   Labor Costs Cycling

A people-oriented approach is needed to solve the problem of labor costs. The solution must recognize that the employees in the factory are in a much better position to find means of increasing productivity than industrial engineers or outside consultants. Workers know where materials are being wasted. They know about methods and machinery changes that will have a tremendous impact on productivity. But they keep this knowledge to themselves, because there is no incentive to tell the boss about it.

Suggestion boxes and cost improvement programs may appear successful on the basis of the total dollars saved, but compare the rewards with the savings, and it is easy to see why the workers are not doing the job they are capable of doing. What is needed is an incentive plan that gives the worker a larger reward. More important, the employee should be rewarded not by a token number of dollars (one large company gives a flat $100 regardless of the size of the savings) but by a share in the productivity improvement.

Experience has shown that about $5\frac{1}{2}$ hours of work is the average for an employee during an eight-hour day. The other $2\frac{1}{2}$ hours are lost through unintentional slowdowns, waste, and inefficiency. Some lost time cannot be avoided, but the $5\frac{1}{2}$ hours of productivity could very easily be increased to $6\frac{1}{2}$ hours by more care and attention to the use of materials, supplies, and outside services, and by improved or new production controls, methods, tools, and fixtures. All these ideas and improvements can come from the production workers themselves, but they will volunteer these improvements only if they are rewarded with an increase in wages predicated on the increase in productivity.

Any reduction in productivity must carry with it punishment of a wage cut. A worker's rate of productivity is in reality a minimum that he has set for himself—just the amount needed to keep his job. If he drops below that rate, his punishment is deserved. If the loss of productivity is due to factors over which the workforce has no control, management must absorb the loss.

A 20% increase in productivity can readily be achieved with only a 4% wage increase. Because all the workers share in the rewards, there is no resentment toward innovations that step up production. Figure 6 shows a typical relationship between worker incentives and productivity increase.

In general, this technique is best used in small and medium-sized companies, but it can be adapted to large companies that are heavily decentralized. The technique is actually a device to increase profits, not a cost-reduction method.

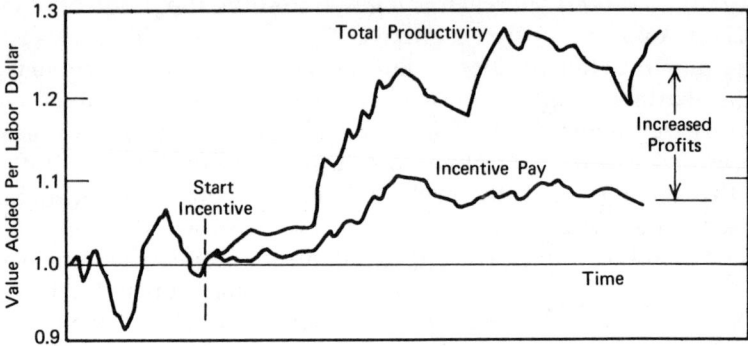

Figure 6   Productivity versus Incentive Pay

CONCLUSIONS

We have demonstrated that the productivity concept, as commonly applied by industrial engineers, is a wholly inadequate approach to improvement of profitability. It is inadequate because it attacks only the visible symptoms without regard for the side effects of the remedy.

Further, no one has yet determined a way to determine the true costs of industrial engineering. Industrial engineering is not wholely amortized by direct labor savings. Until the costs of industrial engineering can be accurately determined, large claims to profit improvement cannot be substantiated.

SUMMARY

The productivity concept of management is an abstraction of the principles of industrial engineering. It is commonly believed that profit is directly related to productivity. The theory is that, if the number of units manufactured is increased by 10% while the cost per unit goes up only 5%, there will be a substantial profit increase.

Cost reduction under this concept is static, a solution for an immediate problem. No attempt is made to foresee and prevent future problems.

Theoretically productivity is output divided by labor. Practically, it is difficult to measure and few companies, even in the same industry, use the same measure. In most cases, productivity is measured by comparison either with past performance or with others in the same industry. So-called engineered standards are based on studies by industrial engineers and thus are historical in nature but, of course, represent the best that can be done.

Learning curves are responsible for the belief that competitiveness is a function of productivity. Industry averages of productivity are also misleading, since the averages mask the true trend. Most of the companies indexed may have had very similar trends.

Industrial engineering is expensive both in initial cost and in the cost of maintaining productivity. Without maintenance, productivity will rapidly deteriorate. Industrial engineering can promise cost reduction but not profit improvement because the impact of reducing direct labor costs on profit is not known.

The productivity concept is a wholly inadequate approach to improvement of profitability. It is inadequate because it attacks only the visible symptoms. In the next chapter a better approach, the profitability concept, will be introduced.

REFERENCES

1. P. Conley, "Experience Curves as a Planning Tool," *IEEE Spectrum*, June 1970, pp. 63–68.
2. S. A. Billon, "Industrial Time Reduction Curves as Tools for Forecasting," *University Microfilms*, Ann Arbor, Mich., 1960.
3. W. B. Hirschmann, "Profit from the Learning Curve," *Harvard Business Review*, 42, Jan.–Feb., 1964, pp. 125–139.
4. F. J. Andress, "The Learning Curve as a Production Tool," *Harvard Business Review*, Jan.–Feb., 1954, pp. 87–97.
5. J. E. Cohen, *Model of Simple Competition*, Harvard University Press, Cambridge, Mass., 1966.
6. Frederick W. Taylor, *The Principles of Scientific Management*, Harper & Bros., New York, 1911.
7. G. R. Gargiulo, "Productivity Analysis," *Management Advisor*, Jan.–Feb., 1974, pp. 23–29.
8. Eric C. Baum, "Industrial Engineering Approaches to Boost Plant Productivity," Productivity Conference, National Productivity Commission, Chicago, Ill., May 23, 1972.
9. J. B. Lathrop, "Bayesianism and Utility," AIAA 3rd Annual Meeting, Boston, Ma., Nov. 1966, AIAA Paper #66-897.
10. H. Chernoff and L. E. Moses, *Elementary Decision Theory*, Wiley, New York, 1959.

CHAPTER 2

THE PROFITABILITY CONCEPT

The primary function of management is producing a profit. Yet most management texts deal with productivity and costs and mention profit only as something peripheral that will result from good management. It is curious that financial statements never use the word "profit". The statements use the terms "income", "earnings", and "revenue". Only the initiated know which refer to company profits. Annual reports do mention profits in their texts but in nebulous terms. A typical report reads:

"Most phases of the Company's business contributed to an increase in operating income. Worker productivity increased during the year, and management was able to control various phases of operating costs. The profitability of operating locations was also increased through an extensive program of location upgrading."

PROFITABILITY

Profit has several meanings in the business context. Profit is the return received on a business undertaking after all operating expenses have been met. It is also the increase in the net worth of a business enterprise in a given accounting period, and there are other definitions not general enough to be pertinent to this discussion.

In addition profit has different meanings to different members of the business community. To some, liquidity is important. They want to see hard dollars remaining in the company accounts after all cost, charges, and fees are paid. They are not concerned with the growth of the firm, even though investors may be very much interested in the net worth and growth.

Liquidity is necessary in order to meet the payroll and other operating expenses. Growth is necessary to attract capital, the lifeblood of the organization. Management must satisfy both requirements and recognize that growth and profit are very much interdependent.

Profitability is best defined as the quality of possessing an operating profit which contributes to the growth of the company. A company that is not growing is not profitable even if its bottom line is consistently in the black. Conversely a growth company can show a loss and still be considered profitable. A company might be losing money because of investments and changes that are necessary to ensure growth. Thus, making manufacturing more efficient will have very little effect on the overall company profits. Increasing productivity rarely affects company growth. It may possibly inhibit it, and it will be deleterious if management believes that improved productivity equates with improved profitability and does nothing to ensure company growth.

The profitability concept is superior to the productivity concept because it is concerned with all elements of profitability. For example, under the profitability concept, management might consider investing in a new product instead of industrial engineering for an old product because of better growth possibilities and eventually higher profits.

MEASURING PROFITABILITY

Productivity can be measured. Costs can be determined easily. Profits on sales are not too difficult to measure. But profitability, as we have defined it, is not directly measurable. One reason is that growth is a rate, actually an acceleration. The company's net worth is increasing at so many dollars per year. Some of this increase may be inventory. There are, however, major questions to be answered. Can the company ever realize a profit on all of its inventory? What are the economic or other forces acting to decelerate the growth?

Profit, on the other hand, is measured in dollars. It is a factor in profitability, and, somehow, it must be related to other factors not measured in dollars. The *Profitability Index* relates profits, sales volume, dollar investment, and time.

$$\text{Profitability Index (PI)} = \frac{\text{Volume (Units)} \times (\text{Unit Price} - \text{Unit Cost})}{\text{Investment (\$)} \times \text{Time}}$$

Profit is represented by the difference between the unit price and the unit cost. Note that productivity is measured by the unit cost. If the

PI is calculated for a one year period, then the indices can be plotted on an annual basis, and the profitability can be monitored. Profitability can be forecast by using market research estimates of the volume.

The index is basically the discounted cash flow technique developed by the Honeywell Company to determine the after-tax return on the investment in a new product development. Honeywell used it to measure engineering performance by using constant unit price and volume. We can use it to measure company and product performance by employing actual prices, volume, and costs. Replacing investment with the net worth of the company, we now have a measure of the impact of a specific product on the profitability of the company.

Example: Carnahan & Jacobs, Inc., make transformers for the aerospace industry. The net worth of the company is $1.5 million, and they have been growing at the rate of 2% a year. The company has been offered a contract to make a special transformer. The customer has indicated that he will purchase 1000 a year for 3 years at $25 each. The engineering and production managers estimated that development and factory unit costs would be $17. The company controller estimated that the company investment in the product would be $100,000 a year. The product PI was calculated as

$$\text{Product PI} = \frac{3000 \times (25 - 17)}{100,000 \times 3} = \frac{24,000}{300,000} = 0.08$$

This was four times the company growth rate and the company agreed to accept the contract.

This decision proved to be rash, because the actual unit cost was $24, and the engineering and production budget was overrun by $25,000. The product PI was than

$$\frac{3000 \times (25 - 24)}{375,000} = \frac{3000}{375,000} = 0.008$$

Note that there was a profit, albeit a small one, but the $3000 profit is offset by a loss of the 2% normal gain on the $125,000 annual investment in this product. The loss is 3 × $2500 or $7500 making the net loss, $4500.

GROWTH RATE

Growth rate can be measured by examining the balance sheets of a company. The balance sheets tabulate both the assets and the

TABLE 2.1   JOHN SMITH COMPANY BALANCE SHEET DATA

($ million)	1976	1975	1974[a]	1973	1972	1971	1970
Asset	32.1	29.5	26.3	30.1	26.8	24.2	23.0
Liabilities	12.1	11.1	9.0	9.0	8.2	8.0	7.8

[a] Inventory value changed by conversion from FIFO to LIFO.

liabilities. Since they are "balance" sheets, the liabilities are made to equal the assets exactly by listing shareholders' equity as part of the liabilities. If the shareholders' equity is omitted, the difference between the remaining liabilities and the total assets equals the net worth of the company.

Assets include items such as receivables and inventories. For that reason, assets may jump upward or downward in years when these are reevaluated, because of new accounting methods or a change in the business environment. These variations must be taken into account when measuring the growth rate. Growth rate is found by comparing net worth for a given year with that of a previous year.

Example: The balance sheets for the John Smith Company provide the data of Table 2.1 (liabilities do not include shareholders' equity).

As an example of the computation involved, the net worth for 1975 is $18.4 million and, for 1976, it is $20.0 million, a gain of $1.6 million. The growth rate was, therefore, 1.6/18 or 8.6%. Figure 7 plots both the net worths and the growth.

The growth curve between 1972 and 1973 reflects the slowdown of the general economy. The period between 1973 and 1974 indicates a drop in net worth due to an accounting change. The growth curve at 1975 implies a very serious problem existed in 1974 that could not have been due to the accounting change. The growth rate was only 4% in 1975 indicating a probable negative rate in 1974. The improvement in the economy in 1975–6 can be seen in both curves. One can only guess at the problem in 1974, but it is safe to say that an increase in productivity was probably not the best solution, since the depressed economy was responsible for lowered demand.

The profitability index can be computed with the help of the statement of earnings. We would use the net profits for the combined sales volume of all the products manufactured and assume that all of the

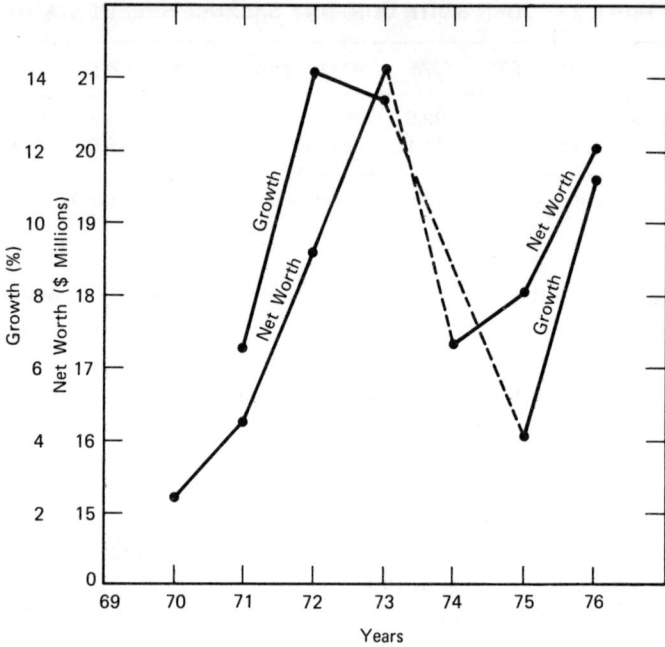

Figure 7   Net Worth and Growth for John Smith Co.

net worth is invested in the products. This PI will serve as a rough measure of the overall profitability of the company.

If a problem is indicated, then it will become necessary to use cost account data to determine the PI for each product and model of a product. The calculation of the PI is accomplished in the following manner:

$$PI = \frac{Profits}{Net\ Worth} = \frac{\$2.2\ million}{\$20.0\ million} = 0.11$$

Example: The earnings statements of the John Smith Company provided the supplementary data of Table 2.2.

Over 30% decline in the profitability index is a flag alerting management to a problem. The first step is to use cost accounting data to determine whether the problem lies in a single product or is company-wide.

Example: Given ten thousand units of a product can be sold at a unit profit of $5 in which $100,000 would have to be invested.

TABLE 2.2 JOHN SMITH COMPANY EARNINGS DATA

(*$ Million*)	1976	1975	1974
Total sales	9.4	8.6	8.0
Total Profits	2.2	2.9	2.4
From Balance Sheet:			
Net Worth	20.0	18.0	17.3
Computed PI	0.11	0.16	0.14
Change	−31.2%	14.3%	—

The problem is to determine the number of units that would have to be sold if the unit profit dropped to $3.75.

$$PI = (\$5 \times \$100{,}000)/\$100{,}000 = 0.5$$
$$0.5 = \$3.75X/\$100{,}000$$
$$X = 13{,}333 \text{ units}$$

This is the volume at a unit profit of $3.75 that would give exactly the same PI as the $5 unit profit. It would be advisable to increase the volume to, say, 20,000 units, in order to bring up the dollar profit. The unit cost and, possibly, the investment may increase by producing the higher volume. But, if these dollars can be controlled sufficiently, a higher profitability will be obtained.

PROBABILISTIC FACTORS (1)

The Carnahan & Jacobs example demonstrates the uncertainty with which managers must deal in most of their decisions. The profitability concept is not exempt from this problem, particularly where estimates of future earnings are involved. Such estimates seriously affect the company's securities on the stock market and, also, management decisions on capital investments.

Budgets are plans incorporating forecasted performance levels. The uncertainty in the forecasts is best treated in terms of risk. Risk can often be minimized by collecting data which is more reliable than the subjective guesstimates of the company's management. Or a probabilistic approach can be used and the highest probability (lowest risk) values selected to support decisions. The latter may be the only path open. Techniques are available that can reduce the risk in the probabilistic approach to a low level.

TABLE 2.3 SUPERIOR CARTS COMPANY PROFIT BUDGET

	Optimistic	Pessimistic	Most	Likely
Sales @ $40/unit		$160,000	$200,000	$228,000
Variable Cost				
Manufacturing		70,000	90,000	100,000
Marketing		10,000	15,000	20,000
Short Run Fixed Costs				
Manufacturing		2,000	4,500	5,500
Marketing		700	750	1,000
Administration		6,000	9,000	10,000
Plant Fixed Costs				
Manufacturing		25,000	25,000	25,000
Marketing		3,000	3,000	3,000
Administration		9,000	9,000	9,000
Profit Before Taxes		34,300	43,750	54,500
Taxes @ 50%		17,150	21,875	27,250
Profit After Taxes		17,150	21,875	27,250

Example: The Superior Carts Company had a new product, a shopping cart. A profit budget was being prepared for the year ending 1978. Breakeven analysis and cost-volume-profit analysis was used to determine the feasibility of the budget. Based on the cost estimates of the various company departments the profit budget was as shown in Table 2.3.

The usual procedure is to publish the most likely figures, because it is believed that they are based on the best estimates of the managers. Superior's president, Sam Daniels, decided he would like to have probabilities and confidence levels assigned to each of the three profit levels. Typical of the data supplied him by this method was that the profit would be $17,926 with a confidence level of 99%, and, with 60% confidence, the profit would be $19,924. These figures were not very helpful to Daniels. Uncertainty still existed. More important, Daniels needed to know which of the estimated profits to use in his planning.

What he needed was some kind of average of the three estimates. The solution was to calculate the average by this formula:

$$\text{Average Profit} = \frac{o + 4m + p}{6}$$

where o = optimistic estimate
      m = most likely estimate
      p = pessimistic estimate

The average is not the most probable with a confidence level of 50%. The average has in its favor that it heavily weights the most likely value but is still affected by the other less likely estimates. The average profit for the shopping carts was computed to be

$$\frac{27,250 + 4(21,875) + 17,150}{6} = \$21,983$$

On the basis of this result, Daniels observed that the most likely estimate would be adequate for his planning. The optimistic estimate did not offer sufficient added profit to compensate for the higher risk. The risk of the pessimistic value being correct did not seriously affect the anticipated profit.

CUSTOMER PROFITABILITY (2)

A quite common problem is that of continued sales volume increases, accompanied by a decline in profits. A great part of this problem at the moment is due to inflation, but there is a more fundamental cause, one that can be controlled.

Accounting systems for cost controls tend to be oriented toward the product line or manufacturing plan, rather than oriented toward the customer. This is responsible for cost averaging. Increasing sales volume often means taking on marginal customers or markets. As a result, total profits are hurt, because each additional sale means increased direct production costs. That is, the product profitability is lower because of higher costs for the marginal customers.

For example, all costs connected with sales, service, and delivery of products are traditionally treated as indirect overhead.

In reality, all these costs are not fixed, nor are they necessarily overhead. Because customers vary in size and location, the cost of servicing them can differ as much as 20% or more. Management needs better information on customer characteristics in order to establish goals based on the most profitable business mix. Customer-oriented marketing strategies can be developed to achieve these goals. Optimum distribution systems can be developed, and there can be more accurate financial planning. There are many organizations that have developed computer programs for costing either individual customers or a marketing area. These are merely highly specialized cost accounting systems. Their cost can be quickly amortized by increased profitability through more selective marketing and/or pricing. Profit improvement through reshaping of the profitability of the business mix is generally *many times larger than that obtainable from improved efficiency alone.*

Conventional accounting systems charge back revenues and costs to a cost center. If the cost center is unprofitable, it is difficult to turn it around, because it is not possible to determine whether the product itself is unprofitable or whether the costs for specific customers are too high. It is quite possible that a different customer mix might present a brighter profit picture.

Identifying unprofitable customers requires an analysis of the product mix, sales coverage, pricing, order profiles, and distribution costs for specific markets and customers. When it has been determined that a customer or customers will never yield a profit, steps can be taken to correct the situation. The customers may be dropped, or corrections may be made in pricing, marketing, and distribution strategies. At the same time, these strategies can be reconstructed to make the profitable market more profitable.

Customer profitability analysis is needed if:

1. Cost centers consistently show lower profits compared to similar operations.
2. Campaigns to increase sales volume are successful, but at lowered profits.
3. The company is serving a substantial customer mix with a uniform marketing strategy.
4. Small orders make up the major portion of the sales volume.

Typical items that can be uncovered by a customer profitability analysis include:

1. A sales force calling on hundreds of customers when the gross margins do not pay for the cost of the call, the processing of the order, and the delivery of the product.
2. Door-to-door delivery to a myriad of small customers in one area. A trade-off study might show that the market might be made profitable if a warehouse or a distributor were set up in the area.
3. Customers whose purchases are large on an annual basis but take delivery in small quantities over the year.

Inventory and freight costs are far too high for such customers. It may be less costly to ship large quantities and wait for payment. Accounts receivable are valuable for obtaining cash. Inventory is just a cost.

The factors to be considered in a customer profitability analysis are order size profiles, customer size and characteristics, special customer requirements, special packaging or handling, product line differences, inventory turnover, and quantity and quality of customer services.

It is not necessary to analyze all the customers separately. Usually it is possible to select a specific market or a specific product. The candidate or candidates for the analysis will depend on the company and the nature of its business. Analysis of one or two customers should yield sufficient data to make it possible to restructure the cost center's policies and procedures to handle all similarly situated customers.

The steps to follow in such an analysis follow:

1. Select a market that is representative of the problem.
2. Choose a finite sampling period.
3. Measure the actual gross revenue from each transaction for a typical customer or customers.
4. Identify all costs for the sales volume during the same period.
5. Perform a sensitivity analysis to determine the most critical costs.
6. Evaluate the impact on profitability of changes in distribution methods, order size mix, service levels, and selling methods.
7. Define strategies for getting customers to accept the changes.
8. Test and evaluate these strategies, as well as the desired changes in the methods.
9. Implement the changes.
10. Plan for introducing the strategies that are successful in other markets.

Example: The Clover Baking Company produced specialty breads and rolls. They supplied a large spectrum of markets throughout the Los Angeles metropolitan area. Their ethnic breads (Greek, Italian, French, etc) were in great demand, but their profits were not as high as standard breads. An examination of one large market failed to give a clue in the profit mystery. The company then analyzed a half-dozen of their customers, making comparisons of order size, service, levels, and selling methods. They found that they had been applying the same selling methods (demonstrators and special displays) to all their customers regardless of order size. The demand for ethnic breads varied considerably with the communities in which the markets were located. As a result, the cost of sales, in some areas, exceeded the sales volume. Clover decided to eliminate the special campaigns for the ethnic breads and concentrate on their other products. The impact on the profits far exceeded their expectations.

Example: The aerospace and defense industries seem unlikely areas for customer profitability analysis, but it can be applied to these industries with highly beneficial results. The Gary Jones Company produced electronics for the military. It was successful in competition with the larger competitors because of the creativity of its engineers, the high efficiency of its factory, and its exceptional marketing personnel. In the field of communications, in spite of underbidding the competition, the company was substantially profitable. The company had recently entered into competition for electronic warfare equipment and systems contracts. The reason for entering this market was an invention developed by company engineers that was thought to be a breakthrough in the state-of-the-art.

The Gary Jones Company appropriated $25,000 for marketing and succeeded in winning a contract, on an unsolicited proposal, for a feasibility study. The contract was for $10,000, which would not even cover the cost of performing the study, let alone any part of the marketing. Upon successful completion of the study, the company found that they had only won the right to be accepted as a bidder on the next large procurement. This meant an additional marketing investment in an uncertain market. With no experience in such systems, the company did not know whether they could profitably underbid the competition.

An initial analysis showed their investment would be:

Engineering	
Development	$100,000
Pre-proposal	100,000
Feasibility	15,000
Marketing	
Initial	25,000
Proposal	50,000
Total	$290,000
Less study contract	10,000
	$280,000

There was no assurance that the company could win a large system contract. Was the gamble worthwhile? If successful, the company could penetrate a billion dollar market and possibly capture a good share of it. If they failed, the loss would be $280,000. Unfortunately the big payoff was too attractive. The Gary Jones proposal was the best it had ever produced and featured the new technique its engineers had developed. However, its fine proposal was not the winner.

If the Gary Jones Company had performed a customer profitability analysis it would have discovered that each of the top competitors had invested $2–5 million to establish themselves in this market. These sums were spent over a period of many years. A new company could never catch up, no matter how much money it was willing to spend. In any case, the return on investment for a latecomer could never be attractive.

PROFITABILITY VERSUS PRODUCTIVITY

The chief difference between these concepts is in the level at which they are applied. Profitability deals with company financial statements, both company-wide and in cost center and product status reports. Productivity is concerned with unit costs. Productivity treats the product as though it were somehow isolated from the body of the company and is the company. All departments dealing with the factory are subservient to the factory, and their sole purpose is nourishing the product. Profit is assumed to come with high efficiency.

Profitability, on the other hand, gives a different purpose to the product, the growth of the company. All departments, not just the factory, exist to further growth. Profit alone is not growth. The rate of profit increase is a measure of growth. *A company showing a loss in its annual report can still have high profitability, despite low productivity.*

There are many cases of companies on the verge of or in bankruptcy that have made complete turnarounds. A recent example is the Memorex Corporation. In 1975, Memorex was on the verge of bankruptcy. In 1977, Memorex reported substantial earnings for the first quarter, with indications of continued growth. There are few companies that have not shown a loss in the first few years of their existence. Those with good profitability have survived and blossomed. The most important difference between productivity and profitability is that productivity deals with *men and machines,* while profitability deals with *dollars and profits.*

SUMMARY

Growth and profit are very much interdependent. Profitability is best defined as the quality of possessing an operating profit contributing to the growth of the company. Profitability is not directly measurable. A measure which relates profit, sales volume, investment, and time is the Profitability Index (PI).

$$PI = \frac{\text{Volume(Units)} \times (\text{Unit Price(\$)} - \text{Unit Cost(\$)})}{\text{Investment(\$)} \times \text{Time}}$$

Productivity enters into this index through the unit cost.

Growth rate can be measured by examining the balance sheets of the company. If the shareholders' equity is omitted, then the difference between the remaining liabilities and the total assets equals the net worth of the company. Allowance must be made for changes in accounting methods or changes in the business environment. The growth rate is found by comparing the net worth for a given year with a previous year.

The overall profitability of the company can be computed from the statement of earnings. The statement shows the profit, which is used with the net worth from the balance sheet to compute the Profitability Index.

The profitability concept is not exempt from the problem of dealing in uncertainities, such as forecasts of performance. Commonly, three estimates are available—optimistic, most likely, and pessimistic. An average of the three can be obtained with a confidence level equal to 50% (an even chance of being correct) by:

$$\text{Average} = \frac{o + 4m + p}{6}$$

where o = optimistic estimate
m = most likely estimate
p = pessimistic estimate

Customer profitability analysis is needed if sales volume increases but profit decreases. Changes in marketing and distribution can correct this problem.

The next chapter will introduce Dynamic Cost Reduction as an application of the Profitability Concept.

REFERENCES

1. R. J. Tersine and C. A. Altimus Jr., "Probabilistic Profit Planning," *Management Adviser*, May–June, 1974, pp. 46–50.
2. M. J. Davoust, "Customer Profitability Analysis," *Management Adviser*, May–June, 1974, pp. 15–19.

CHAPTER 3

DYNAMIC COST REDUCTION (DCR)

Most companies devote considerable time and effort to cost accounting and control, the measurement and correction of the performance of the individual compartments of the company and its managers. To be effective, cost control needs goals and plans in the form of operating budgets or cost standards. The measurement compares operating costs with the operating budgets and/or cost standards to flag variances so that corrective action can be taken. Thus, cost control is concerned with keeping costs below established standards under existing conditions.

Industrial cost reduction efforts, in the past, have been limited to one-shot programs that were dropped when the crisis had passed. This, *static cost reduction,* stems from an addiction to the productivity concept. Recently, it has become quite common for companies (and even industries) to become noncompetitive. The industries, particularly consumer electronics, were unable to compete with foreign producers. The cost reduction programs followed one another as rapidly as the crises developed. This was still static cost reduction, because it was concerned with reducing costs to the level of established standards. In these cases, the *standards were established by the competition, not by the profitability requirements of the company. Dynamic Cost Reduction,* on the other hand, is concerned with reducing costs but allowing flexible standards. These standards are related to the profitability of the company and vary as the market for the product varies. The standards can be developed by subtracting the goal profit from the product's unit selling price.

STATIC COST REDUCTION

The dramatic difference between static and dynamic cost reduction is best illustrated by an actual case.

An industrial engineer was called to increase the profit for a machined product. The obvious industrial engineering approach was to examine manufacturing costs for possible savings. However, these were among the initial conditions:

1. No specific profit goal was established.
2. No specific cost goal was established.

The industrial engineer, typically, worked at unit cost reduction on the premise that lowered unit cost would permit higher profits. He determined that the breakdown of the product cost was similar to Figure 8.

The industrial engineer knew he could achieve no more than 10% improvement in production labor costs, because of the high efficiency of the factory. He felt that the maximum cost-cutting potential existed in materials handling, where a new computer program for optimizing material handling costs could be instituted. (1)

Materials handling involves moving materials into and out of the company and between company operations. A large number of people

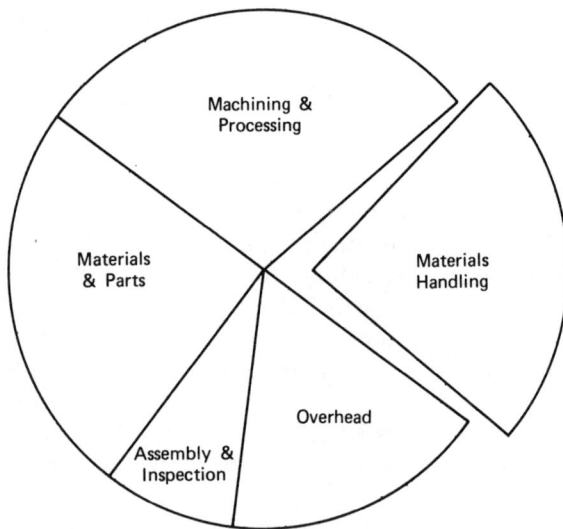

Figure 8   Breakdown of Product Cost

do nothing but handle and move material full time. Added to this number are support personnel—clerks, supervisors, and material handling maintenance people. Materials handling costs are further increased by lost direct labor dollars, because workers are required to handle materials rather than produce. Better handling methods can reduce this. This means a study of the operation to determine the ratio of time spent on handling to operation time.

The study in this case showed that the direct labor handling loss ratio was:

$$\frac{\% \text{ Time Handling} \times \text{Dept. Payroll}}{\text{Dept. Payroll}} = 86{,}580/655{,}000 = 0.132$$

This figure was low, but by reducing it to about 0.05, \$35,000 a year could be saved.

The materials handling labor ratio was

$$\$178{,}160/\$655{,}000 = 0.272$$

It did not appear difficult to reduce this ratio to 0.15, producing a saving of about \$80,000. Total estimated savings then would be \$115,000 in direct labor cost. This meant a reduction of 17.5% in unit cost.

Since the only direction given the industrial engineer was to cut costs sufficiently to amortize his fee within one year, he was congratulated on his success. His fee of \$30,000 was amortized in about four months (one month to implement improvements, plus three months of savings at \$9580 per month).

One obvious fallacy was in the amount of the savings. The actual cost reduction for the first year was \$115,000 − \$30,000 = \$85,000. This means the cost reduction was only 12.9% for the first year. Because 5% per year would have to be spent each year to maintain the improvements, the cost reduction remained at the 12.9% level.

The first problem that presents itself here is that of additional, necessary cost reductions. Note that no more than 10% reduction can be achieved in nonmaterial-handling operations. If the 10% saving can be achieved at a cost of 5%, then only 5% of the direct labor cost can be cut. This may not be adequate. What to do? The "what" will be some drastic measures that may seriously affect the morale and the profitability of the company. For example, union contract negotiations may be stymied by the problem of increasing wages while maintaining profits in a highly competitive industry.

The DCR approach differs from static cost reduction by defining company profit goals and the current market price. The difference between the two is the product cost standard. We will return to this type of problem for a DCR solution after a discussion of the details of a DCR program.

PROFITABILITY GOALS

The first and most important step in developing a DCR program is setting the profit goals. The success or failure of the program depends on whether the goals are achievable and acceptable to all with an interest in the enterprise. The number of goals differ with the size and the character of each firm.

The roster of goals that are needed includes:

1. Growth rate for the company.
2. Profitability index for the company.
3. Profitability index for each product.
4. Profit rate for each product.

All goals must be based on industry experience, investors requirements, and management's expertise. The procedure for setting goals varies with each industry and the company and, of course, with whether the organization is well established or just starting. Although the procedure may vary, the benefits from setting profit goals will not.

For example, after company goals have been established, the feasibility of achieving these goals with planned or present products becomes immediately visible. Excessive optimism and enthusiasm can very well deprive management of this important advantage. Industry experience and management skills should provide reasonable bounds for expectations. Managers cannot expect to find some unique production technique or novel design at some later time that will permit achievement of their goals. The wild enthusiasm of investors caused by an industry boom should not mislead managers into setting unreasonable goals, especially growth rate goals. Caution and the use of pessimistic estimates is advisable.

In setting profit goals, no attempt should be made to take into consideration the efficiency of the company or the current selling price for the products. The purpose of the goals is to determine what the company needs not only to survive, but also to grow at a reasonable rate. If, when the program plan is completed, it is found that the profit goals can never be achieved, then it will be necessary to make a change, probably a radical one. There are no degrees of feasibility. Either the company has a bright and viable future or none at all. A flat, no-growth future is a sure path to the bankruptcy courts.

Most companies measure their growth by the dollar volume of sales. This is a very misleading index because it gives no indication of how much earnings contribute to the growth. Sales volume may be due to an unusual, temporary demand or an inflationary price for the product.

Only an increase in net worth can measure the true profitability. A case in point is the Hewlett-Packard Company. The company is an extremely well managed electronic instrument manufacturer. From 1972 to 1973, its sales grew 38%. In 1974, this growth was slowed to about 20%. The 1974 profit on sales was about 8%. This figure is much higher than the rest of the large electronics companies and is very nearly the same as the company's peak earnings in 1966. However, because 1973 was a boom year for the industry, component shortages were responsible for delivery stretchouts. Cash flow was reduced because of equipment in inventory and the need for dollars for raw materials.

Hewlett-Packard was forced, like others in the industry, into short-term borrowing at high interest rates to support its growth. The 1973 ratio between interest expense and sales was twice the 1966 figure. The only solution was to cut the interest cost at the expense of growth. Growth in this case was measured by sales volume. The moral of this tale is that sales volume is a poor measure of growth.

Another example was the method used by several large circulation magazines to bolster their falling profitabilities. The magazine found the solution by *reducing their circulation.* Editorial and printing costs were the same, no matter what the size of the circulation, but the costs of producing and distributing the publications rose faster than the circulation. Costs of delivery to subscribers were directly proportional to the number of subscribers, and distribution to newstands was much more economical. Revenue from advertising depended to some extent on the circulation. Subscriptions covered only a small portion of the magazine costs. By reducing the circulation, costs dropped with only a small decrease in revenue from advertising. In essence, the magazines were experiencing a negative incremental gain. They cut back to the point where the operations were profitable.

Other industries have used the same technique. In one case a company reduced the number of models produced. In another the number of customers was reduced.

GROWTH RATE GOAL

Company consolidated balance sheets make an excellent source of information for setting this goal. For each year, the difference between the assets and liabilities is the net worth of the company. The liabilities, of course, do not include shareholders' equity. Care must be taken to have all items stated in the same terms each year. For example, inventory should be consistently based on either cost or market value and either the LIFO and FIFO method. For instance:

TABLE 3.1   CONSOLIDATED BALANCE SHEET, THE VEGA CORPORATION

Sept. 30	1976	1975
Current Assets		
Cash	$ 3,100,000	$ 2,430,000
Short-term investm.	4,739,000	7,010,000
Trade receivables	4,006,000	4,254,000
Inventories	3,816,000	2,189,000
Deferred taxes	1,250,000	1,739,000
Property, Plant and Equipment		
Land and buildings	2,604,000	1,944,000
Rental machines	23,900,000	20,986,000
Deprec. allowances	(12,988,000)	(11,700,000)
Other Assets	1,757,000	800,000
Total Assets	$32,193,000	$29,652,000
Current Liabilities		
Notes payable	$ 1,177,000	$ 547,000
Accounts payable	1,948,000	1,141,000
Accrued expenses	1,508,000	1,089,000
Taxes payable	1,726,000	3,123,000
Employee Benefits	2,049,000	1,717,000
Total Liabilities	$ 8,408,000	$ 7,617,000

```
1975 net worth = $22,035,000
1976 net worth =  23,785,000
     Increase =   1,750,000
       Growth =       7.9%
```

Inflation seriously affects some of the items in the balance sheet, but, in general, it affects both assets and liabilities equally. Inflation, therefore, can be discounted in this computation. The Hewlett-Packard profit situation demonstrated that the growth goal had to be based on the current business environment and not on past history. This means

**TABLE 3.2   CONSOLIDATED STATEMENT OF
EARNINGS OF THE VEGA CORPORATION**

Sept. 30	1976	1975
Revenues		
Sales	$ 9,409,000	$ 8,569,000
Services	14,546,000	14,978,000
Other	274,000	330,000
Total Revenues	$24,229,000	$23,877,000
Costs and expenses		
Cost of products	$ 5,378,000	$ 5,305,000
Cost of services	4,477,000	4,241,000
Selling & G&A	11,006,000	9,896,000
Total Expenses	$20,861,000	$19,442,000
Net	3,368,000	4,435,000
Company Profit Rate	16.1%	22.0%

that the growth rate must be re-examined each year and adjustments made to fit economic conditions—change in product mix, change in inventory costing, changes in government control, and changes in taxes.

The remaining profit goals are examined in the Statement of Earnings, Table 3.2.

Some interesting information can be obtained from the statement of earnings. The company's profit rate has dropped almost 6%, although the company's net worth has increased at the rate of 8%. The rather high profit rate, 16–20%, accounts for this. This leads to a suspicion that the 8% growth rate goal may be too low. Further, profit rates can be calculated:

	1976	1975
Products	−2.7%	−6.5%
Services	65%	45%

These were calculated by proportioning the selling and G&A costs according to the revenues for each item.

It is obvious that the services are compensating for the products' losses and are responsible for all the company's growth. There is a clue as to the disproportionate figures. The selling and G&A costs are extremely high, about 50% of the revenues. A more reasonable figure might be 10%.

Recalculating the profit rates with only 10% of revenues for selling cost gives:

	1976	1975
Products	48%	39%
Services	145%	160%
Company	97%	100%

These profit rates may be extremely optimistic, because we do not know enough about the operation to determine whether 10% selling costs are feasible. More realistic profit goals lie somewhere between the two profit rates. Tabulating the 1976 figures shows:

Percent of Selling Costs	10	50	Average Profit Rate
Products	48%	−2.7%	25%
Services	145%	+65%	105%
Company	97%	16.1%	56%

The averages are the profit goals. It must be remembered that these are tentative goals and are subject to revision when proven unrealistic. Goal growth can now be revised. The company profit rate for 1976 was 16.1%. The goal profit rate is 56%. This is a 71% increase. Therefore the goal growth rate can be increased by the same amount, making the new goal, 13.7%.

This is an example of a situation where a full DCR program is not needed. If approached from productivity, the low profit on the manufactured products would have received the full attention of the industrial engineers. Note that an increase of productivity as high as 50% would have had only a slight effect on the company's profit picture. Yet merely going through the exercise of setting profitability goals has pinpointed the real problem, sales costs. Observe that a 50% decrease in that cost produced an 1800% increase in the products' profit and a 120% increase in the profit on services. The high profit rate for services masked the problem by giving the company the appearance of high profitability even though it was losing money on the manufactured products.

PRICING

In the Vega Corporation example, the pricing of the products was not important. In most other cases, the unit price is needed, because the difference between the price and the goal profit is the goal cost.

Adding the goal profit to the estimated cost of producing the article will not do, at least not in today's highly competitive markets. It can be done when supplying the military with weapons systems but, even there, the DCR approach can mean more winning proposals because of lower prices.

The cost of an intensive, in-depth market research program is minute compared to the serious damage that will result from failure to purchase such a program. The purpose of market research is to remove uncertainties. Probabilistic market research programs, such as sampling, substitute one kind of uncertainty for another. Samplings of a market require statistical analysis to project the whole market. This projection is based on probability theory. The theory is reasonably sound only if the sampling is truly random. There is no known technique for assuring the researcher of a random sample of a given market. Thus the guesstimate of any experienced marketeer is just as reliable as the statistical analysis result. (2)

Sampling studies performed by trade magazines consist of mailing questionaires to subscribers. Rarely do these mailings reach sufficient people who buy or specify. Most of those who do respond are not involved in procurement. Similarly, research done by consultant organizations use Poor's and similar directories. The information available in such directories is too skimpy and inaccurate to be useful for market research.

Recommended sources for pricing information are:

1. Component vendors who can give information about the competitions' purchasing policies—prices, quantities, deliveries, types, and the like. Most suppliers are quite willing to give this information since it helps them with their sales.
2. Industry associations, which have a great deal of data plus some good projections and forecasts.
3. Federal agencies that are in the business of collecting industrial statistics. There is an amazing amount of valuable information available without cost or for a nominal fee.
4. Ethical and professional market research organizations that publish reports. These are not expensive compared with studies done privately for a firm. Needed is assurance that the research organization is an ethical one and that the data is accurate.
5. Wholesalers, retailers, and other distributors—the people who will be selling a company's product and who should have a voice in its pricing exercise.
6. Trade shows and editors of trade magazines.
7. The competition, whose sales people are quite willing to give

price, delivery, and specification information to anyone inquiring about a product.

8. Stockbrokers, whose research departments have excellent background information on whole industries as well as specific companies.
9. Banks.

For DCR programs, pricing must be more than 'competitive'. Competitive implies efficiency equal to that of the competition, and make it possible to sell at approximately the same price. When profit is the concern, several questions arise about pricing by the competition:

1. How profitable is the competition? The profitability concept applies here not productivity.
2. How does the quality of the products compare?
3. How good is the management of the competitors?
4. What new developments are presently in the competitions' laboratories and the component suppliers' laboratories?
5. What is the outlook for prices and delivery of components for the next 5 years?

A company may be able to compete today, but will it be able to compete a year from now or 5 years? If a company is at top efficiency now, what will it do when the competition cuts prices? The five points listed above are intended to provide the basis for proper planning to meet challenges of the competition or changes in the broad economy in the foreseeable future.

Some examples of the fate that befalls those who do not plan in this manner are: digital watches, calculators, and computer peripherals. In each case, attracted by a rich boom, a horde of small companies rushed to compete with the giants who developed the first products. It is axiomatic that the giants are highly inefficient despite fortunes poured into industrial engineering. What is more important, the bureaucracy of a large corporation means extremely high G&A costs.

It is not difficult, therefore, for a small or medium-sized company to compete with the giants, while the demand exceeds the supply. Competing means beating the prices of the large company. When the demand levels off, investments in R.&D. by the giants start to pay off. The small companies find themselves with warehouses filled with products that are higher priced than the new products offered by the large companies.

COST STANDARDS (3)

The cost standards for DCR differ considerably from those for productivity programs. Productivity requires only one set of standards, unit costs. DCR requires two, unit costs and company costs. For example,

Productivity: Unit Profit = Unit Price − Unit Cost.

Unit cost is a function of company productivity and material costs. It is relatively noncontrollable. Material costs are only minimally controlled by the firm. Productivity is bound by the limitations of men and machines. Productivity can be measured, and the control is restricted to correcting deviations. Thus, essentially the unit price determines the unit profit, and the price can only be controlled by companies in a monopolistic situation (i.e. the instant photography industry until recently) or in some government procurements. The unit cost here is the cost standard, a fixed value.

Profitability: Goal Cost = Unit price − Goal Unit Profit.

Instead of fighting the productivity battle and experimenting with purchasing and materials inventory strategies, the manager is asked to try a new approach. A basic question must be answered. At the current market price, what must the unit cost be to obtain the profit needed not only to survive, but also to grow?
Several answers are possible:

1. The goal unit cost is within 10% of what the unit is costing now. This is not a good situation. The profit is at the mercy of productivity and material costs. That is, the control is limited and it is only a question of time before the profit will be squeezed.
2. The goal unit cost is very much lower than the current cost. This is worse than the first answer, but at least it doesn't tempt management to leave things alone. It is proof that a productivity improvement program will not help the situation.
3. It is extremely unlikely that the goal unit cost would ever be very much higher than the current cost. Of course, this is the ideal situation and is, in reality, the ultimate goal of DCR.

The DCR unit cost is the cost standard for the product. But now the base for the standard must be broadened. No longer must it cover only productivity and material costs. Included now must be engineering, marketing, quality assurance, OSHA costs, environmental pollution prevention costs, cost of money, and any other business expenses. Some of these items can not be controlled or reduced. However, many can be tightly controlled, and some can be avoided.

Using the DCR unit cost standard requires an analysis of the costs to determine the effect on the total unit cost of any reduction in each of the cost elements. In the next chapter, some useful techniques for cost analysis and sensitivity analysis will be examined. The cost analysis permits options other than improving productivity. For example, small savings in each of the cost elements (including productivity) may add up to a sizable reduction in the total unit cost. This would make situation number 1 viable in cases where only slight improvement in productivity is feasible.

When the goal unit cost is very much lower than the current cost, cost analysis will determine the feasibility of the standard. If, despite lowering the profit goal, the unit cost standard goal is beyond achievement, a need for dropping or replacing the product is indicated.

The second DCR cost standard is implicit in the profitability index goal. The PI goal is found by dividing the goal profits by the share of the net worth invested in the product. The companywide PI goal depends on the goal growth rate. What this means is that the DCR unit cost standard may be modified, usually downward, in order to ensure the required growth. In practice, the PI goal is not needed for the design of the DCR program. It is better used as a management control tool for monitoring the DCR program. It provides checks for the effectiveness of the program. If the growth is too low, then the cost standards must be lowered.

Example: The Standard Machinery Corporation has one press operation that has been troublesome. It was not profitable when the labor costs were $10 per thousand pieces. The concern's industrial engineers attacked the problem and succeeded in reducing the cost to $6.50 (a 35% reduction). The operation was still losing money.

A DCR approach to this problem would have been as follows:

Goal profit = 50%
Material and other fixed costs = $2/thousand pieces
Price/thousand = $8/thousand
Price − goal profit = goal cost
$8 − $4 = $4 for both labor and materials
$4 − $2 = $2 goal cost for direct labor

It is obvious that no amount of industrial engineering could get the direct labor cost down this far. The recommended solution is to discontinue the operation or, if it is necessary, change the troublesome press or its method of manufacture. This example illustrates that DCR can be applied to a segmented problem as well as to overall company operations. The most important contribution of DCR is the new approach to cost standards.

Up to now, cost standards were recorded of what the product had cost to make and were modified only when the exigencies of the market place demanded it. Such cost standards are used only to verify that a particular operation is maintaining its efficiency. Positive variances, if not too large, are not usually treated with alarm. There is no real motivation for reexamination of the standard unless a crisis occurs.

If DCR cost standards are exceeded, management is very much concerned. That's because the profitability of the company is being affected in a way that is quite visible. The impact on profit for productivity standards variances is not readily determined. Often the effect are not to be felt until many months have passed.

Let us take a DCR approach to the problem posed at the start of this chapter under static cost reduction. With no profitability or cost goals, the industrial engineer addressed himself to production costs. He achieved a 12.9% unit cost reduction.

Assume the unit selling price is determined to be $3.50 and the required profit is $1.00. Then the goal cost is $2.50. Volume is 10,000 units and net worth investment is $100,000. Goal growth rate is 5%. The goal PI is:

$$\frac{\$1 \times 10,000}{\$100,000} = 0.1$$

It is determined that production costs are 40% of the unit costs and that the present unit cost is $2.65. Thus, the unit production cost is $1.06.

The industrial engineer reduced the unit production cost 12.9%, making it $0.92. This reduced the total unit cost to $2.51. The unit cost is approximately equal to the required cost goal.

Unfortunately, although the goals had been met, the net worth increased only 4%. This can be corrected in two ways:

1. The sales volume could be increased 400 units. This probably could be achieved without additional investment. The profit per

unit would remain at $1 giving a net profit of $10,400—$400 above the goal.

2. The preferred approach would be an adjustment of the cost standard downward. This adjustment is only 4¢ to $2.46. The adjustment is small enough to be readily accomplished, requiring no additional investments or sales campaigns. And the profit per unit will be increased to $1.04, resulting in the identical net of $10,400 for only 10,000 units.

DYNAMIC COST REDUCTION (DCR)

With the goals and cost standards set, the next step is to develop a DCR program. The program will vary with the size and nature of the company and its needs. All for-profit companies need DCR, even if the company is prosperous and paying dividends. This prosperity may be false because of undetected problem areas. Greater profits might be realized with DCR. Not-for-profit organizations can benefit from DCR by more efficient utilization of their funds.

DCR can be applied to any of the following situations:

1. Start-ups. A business plan based on DCR should have a better chance of obtaining capital because the plan for company growth is solidly detailed. Without DCR, the investors must guess at the potential and take large risks. A business plan indicating large potential profits does not ensure the growth of the fledgling company. Investors are interested mainly in growth.

2. Company in trouble. Trouble can come in various forms—losing share of market, low profits, losses, poor cash flow, excessive inventory, etc. Regardless of the problem, DCR can pinpoint the trouble and permit remedies to be applied effectively.

3. Profitable company. Profitable companies can benefit from DCR perhaps more than a financially-troubled company. The only recourse for the latter may be bankruptcy. The profitable company with DCR may be able to improve its profits through lowered costs and the bolstered weak areas.

4. Chapter XI companies. The reorganization of such companies can be expedited by the application of DCR. The return to profitability can be quicker and the directions the company should take better defined.

5. One-shot problems. A crisis is at hand. There is no time to initiate a full-blown DCR program. A quickie DCR solution can be obtained as in the Standard Machinery example.

6. Nonprofit organizations. It may appear strange to apply a profitability concept to a nonprofit organization. However, a surplus is equivalent to profit. The profit goal becomes a goal surplus. The price is the allocated funds. The cost standard is the difference between the goal surplus and the budget funds.
7. Special projects. DCR can be profitably applied to the planning of special projects, even such items as relocation of facilities.

The procedure in developing DCR programs is essentially the same in all cases. The steps are:

1. Goal setting.
2. Pricing.
3. Cost standards development.
4. Cost analysis.
5. Cost reduction implementation.
6. Controls implementation.

The details of each step will vary with the application. The procedure is best illustrated by case studies, which will be presented at appropriate points.

An important basic principle of DCR is the minimizing of decisions based on probabilities. (2) Too many management decisions must be made from uncertain premises. It is unfortunate that mathematicians and managers alike have come to accept a probability as a "most likely" outcome. This is far from the truth. The "accuracy" of the probability is a function of an accurate count of the possible outcomes. It is extremely difficult to obtain an accurate count, even with simple devices as a pair of dice.

Because of the limitations on probabilities, DCR techniques are designed to reduce the reliance on probabilities. One example is the recommendations for market research in the pricing discussion.

SUMMARY

Cost reduction is usually a one-shot campaign to cut costs because of a crisis in the marketplace. In such static cost reduction, the cost standards have been established by the competition, not by the profitability requirements of the company. Dynamic Cost Reduction (DCR) is concerned with reducing costs but allowing flexible standards. DCR does not need to set standards and, in fact, can be applied to areas of the business where it is difficult to develop standards such as sales, R&D, maintenance, and facilities. Dynamic Cost Reduction deals with the present company environment, not the past.

These standards are related to the profitability of the company and will vary as the market for the product varies. The standards are developed by subtracting the goal profit from the product's unit selling price.

The first step in a DCR program is setting the profit goals. These are growth rate for the company, profitability index for the company, profitability index for each product, and profit rate for each product.

Good market research is essential to competitive pricing which, in turn, is important to setting cost goals. For DCR, competitive pricing is that price which will permit the company to compete but will, at the same time, further the company goals.

All DCR programs have the same procedural steps, goal setting, pricing, cost standards development, cost analysis, implementation, and control.

The next chapter deals with sensitivity analysis, a very important tool for DCR programs. For this application, sensitivity analysis has been developed in a form that makes it more powerful than the technique as used by accountants.

REFERENCES

1. P. H. Karatassos, "Optimization in Material Handling," (unpublished PHD dissertation, California Western University, 1978).
2. I. Dlugatch, "The Meaning of Probability," Third Conference on Gambling, Las Vegas, Nev., Dec. 1976.
3. J. L. Roth, "Cost Reduction Begins Where Cost Control Ends," *Management Adviser*, May–June, 1974, pp. 32–38.

CHAPTER 4

SENSITIVITY ANALYSIS

A major requirement for efficient cost reduction is establishing the areas to be attacked. All businesses are complex organizations with a multitude of interdependent operations, only a few of which offer any real savings potential. Since cost reduction is not free of cost, it is essential that the savings realized exceed the cost reduction costs sufficiently to justify its application. Thus, selecting areas for cost reduction is most critical. A technique for accurately pinpointing the areas with the greatest payoff is sorely needed. Sensitivity analysis is a practical method for this purpose.

Sensitivity analysis is a technique that measures how the expected values in a decision model will be affected by changes in the data. It is a technique used extensively by accountants to answer such questions as the effect of a change in cash inflows on net-present-value of an investment. In accounting, sensitivity analysis provides an immediate financial measure of the consequences of errors in forecasting. (1)

For the DCR application, sensitivity analysis is an important tool. However, the large company is very complex. A relatively small change in an obscure department could cause a large disturbance in the profitability. For example, a bottleneck in the mail-room may be responsible for delays in processing orders resulting in cancellations, disruption of the production line, and the like.

VALUE ENGINEERING (VE) (2,3)

Value engineering is a technology that is used mainly by the aerospace industry. The Department of Defense views VE as a systematic and creative approach for increasing the investment return on items procured by the Department. This is the same objective as DCR and, for that reason, makes VE of interest for DCR. With modifications, a methodology for VE will be useful to DCR programs.

Value engineering is defined as an organized effort directed at analyzing the function of systems, equipment, facilities, procedures, and supplies for the purpose of achieving the required function at the lowest total cost.

For the productivity concept, cost cutting means reviewing products and their costs. Value engineering, on the other hand, takes nothing for granted. The VE technique evaluates all attributes of a product, including its very existence. Thus, it is focused on the cost effectiveness of products. DCR, like VE, takes nothing for granted and evaluates all attributes of a company, including its very existence.

A major handicap to efficient VE of a large system is establishing the areas to be attacked. Since VE is not free, it is essential that the savings realized through VE exceed its costs sufficiently to justify its application. Thus, the product selection element of VE is critical, and a method for accurately pinpointing the areas with the greatest payoff is important.

For value engineering, the usual first step is to select the most expensive or the most complex subsystem as the most likely subject. The subsystem is then broken down further to find the most expensive subelement and then to apply VE to this subelement. An alternative would be to attack all areas in an attempt to maximize the savings.

Some of the considerations in deciding which way to go are:

1. The analyst has prejudices. If he is a mechanical engineer, he will vote for examining the mechanical components, because he is familiar with them. Note the parallel to industrial engineering. The industrial engineer is usually production-oriented and rarely is interested in the non-manufacturing areas of the company.
2. If large quantities of the product are to be manufactured, then the least expensive item can still yield substantial savings. This is the justification used by industrial engineers for their approach to cost cutting.
3. It is not possible to predict with any accuracy how much cost reduction can be bought with each dollar spent on value engineering. This is not true for industrial engineering since any good industrial engineer can predict to the penny how much unit cost reduction will be achieved. DCR, on the other hand, can predict how much *profit improvement* can be obtained for each dollar saved.

To illustrate this assume an electromechanical product whose total cost is C_T. Figure 9 shows the cost interdependencies for the product.

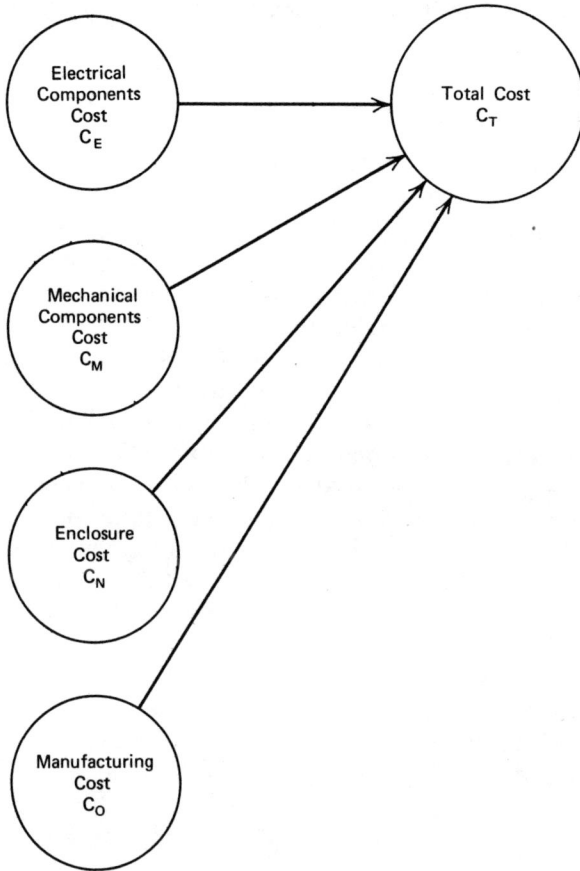

Figure 9   Cost Interdependencies for Product

The total cost is the sum of the four individual costs or

$$C_T = C_E + C_M + C_N + C_O$$

where C_T = total cost
$ C_E$ = electrical components cost
$ C_M$ = mechanical components cost
$ C_N$ = enclosure cost
$ C_O$ = manufacturing cost

A cost analysis determines the following:

$$C_O = 0.09\, C_T$$
$$C_E = 0.31\, C_T$$
$$C_M = 0.52\, C_T$$
$$C_N = 0.08\, C_T$$

The mechanical parts have the greatest potential for savings since they represent 52% of the total cost. A 50% saving here would give a 26% reduction in the total cost. This is more than could be realized from a 50% cost reduction in all three of the remaining functions. However, we may not be able to reduce C_M 50%, and the goal may be something greater than 26%, thus, requiring work on all of the functions. It is necessary to determine the impact of each of the reductions in the other costs on the total costs so that VE dollars will not be wasted on low potential items. Also, it is important to consider the size of the reductions that are feasible. The technique for this analysis is called *sensitivity analysis.* However, this a mathematical technique useful in control system engineering and not the accounting.

For the product in our example, we have the data in Table 4.1.

Assume the goal is to reduce the total costs, C_T, by 35%. There are several ways to accomplish this goal. The best method is to assign reductions to the elements in the order of their potential and to the limits of their feasible reductions. For example, for C_M, maximum reduction possible is 20% and C_M is 52% of the total cost. Therefore:

$$\text{Contribution of } C_M = 0.2 \times 0.52 = 10.4\%$$

Similarly, C_E can save 4.65%; C_O, 2.7%; and C_N, 0.8%. Total savings are 18.55% about half of the goal. It is evident that the goal is too high. Also, these are the ceilings on the individual reductions. There should be some room for error.

TABLE 4.1   COST DATA FOR ELECTROMECHANICAL PRODUCT

	Maximum Feasible Cost Reduction (%)	Share of Total Cost (%)
C_O	30	9
C_E	15	31
C_M	20	52
C_N	10	8

A good approach would be to set as the goals 80% of the maximum feasible reductions. Then:

$$C_O = 0.24 \times 0.09 = 0.022$$
$$C_E = 0.12 \times 0.31 = 0.037$$
$$C_M = 0.16 \times 0.52 = 0.083$$
$$C_N = 0.08 \times 0.08 = \underline{0.006}$$
$$\text{Total} \qquad 0.148$$

The largest possible saving is thus 15%, and it is necessary to reduce the goal to that level.

Another approach is to effect savings only on the parts and make no attempt to reduce manufacturing costs (the enclosure saving is too small to merit expending valuable VE dollars on it). Industrial engineering costs may well be higher than the saving on manufacturing costs. Thus, the goal cost reduction becomes 3.7 plus 8.3 or 12%.

At this point value engineering would be turned off; it can do no more. DCR, however, is concerned with profitability. If the 12% is not sufficient to ensure profitability, then more drastic action is prescribed. In this case, it might be complete redesign or elimination of the product.

Example: The Gerald Company is producing an electromechanical device which is uncompetitive because of its price. It is necessary to find how best to cut costs so that the price can be lowered without affecting profits. The electrical function cost, C_E, is determined by the electrical parts specifications. The mechanical function cost, C_M, is determined by both the electrical parts and the mechanical parts specifications, because the size and shape of the electrical parts will determine the mechanical specifications. The enclosure function cost, C_N, depends not only on all parts specifications but also the case, cover, and fastening specifications. Finally, the production cost, C_P, consists of the parts specifications, labor costs, and the overhead.

The financial records show that the current cost ratios are:

$$C_M/C_E = 1.7$$
$$C_N/C^E = 0.3$$
$$C_P/(C_E + C_M) = 0.1$$
$$C_T = \text{Total Cost} = C_E + C_M + C_N + C_P$$

Cost ratios are established as in Table 4.2.

TABLE 4.2   COST RATIOS

	C_M	C_N	In Terms Of C_P	C_E
C_E	$C_M/1.7$	$C_N/0.3$	$C_P/0.27$	—
C_M	—	$1.7C_N/0.3$	$0.17C_P/0.027$	$1.7C_E$
C_N	$0.3C_M/1.7$	—	$0.3C_P/0.27$	$0.3C_E$
C_P	$0.27C_M/1.7$	$0.27C_N/0.3$	—	$0.27C_E$

From the table the individual costs are found to be as follows:

	$\%C_T$
C_E	31
C_M	52
C_N	8
C_P	9

Then, C_M, with 52% of the total cost is the cost with the greatest potential for savings. It is desired to achieve a 25% total cost reduction.

A 50% saving in C_M achieves a 26% reduction of the total cost. This is more than could be realized from a 50% cost reduction in all three of the remaining costs, but it may not be possible to reduce C_M 50%. Work may be necessary on all the costs. The probable best choice would be to cut from C_E and C_M. To obtain 25% total reduction would require only about 30% reduction of C_E and C_M. A rough estimate of this figure can be computed by $(31 + 52)X = 25$ and $X = 25/83 = 0.3$.

It is obvious that the cost of the mechanical portion of the product can be broken down into two contributing costs, electrical and mechanical part specifications. With only two costs it is a simple matter to establish which of the two has the greatest potential. Less obvious is the fact that the electrical specifications are responsible for 31% of the total cost and represent a major portion of the mechanical costs. Any reduction of the electrical costs would materially affect all other costs. If the mechanical costs were composed of very many factors, an analyst skilled in mathematics would be needed to perform a sensitivity analysis. The use of less complex lower level breakdowns usually can simplify the task.

DCR SENSITIVITY ANALYSIS

The firm is extremely more complex than the simple electromechanical product considered previously. Figure 10 is a representation of the network of the interdependencies of costs in a typical company.

The network represents the interdependency of various areas for sales volume as well as costs. There are no arrowheads for direction of flow. This is because the flow is bidirectional. For example, if the sales volume increases:

Distribution volume and costs increase.
Manufacturing volume and costs increase.
Labor costs increase but not the labor force.
Material costs and volume increase.
Sales costs increase.
G&A dollars increase.

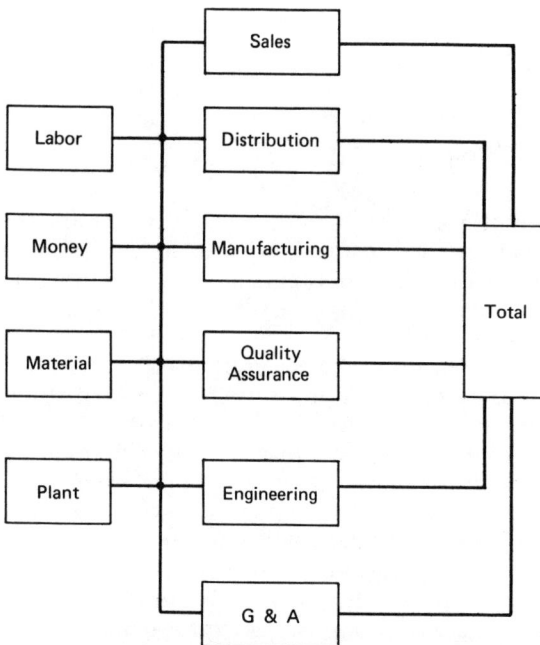

Figure 10   Network Model of the Firm

The increase in sales volume may have been due to reduced manufacturing costs and/or distribution costs, possibly an increase in the labor force or a product improvement at higher engineering cost.

Because of the high complexity of even a small company's interdependencies, it is advisable to borrow one aspect of value engineering methodology, reducing the problem in size by selecting the most expensive area of the business as the target for DCR. The wisdom of this is demonstrated by the electromechanical product example.

Sometimes the most expensive area may be the one in which cost reduction is expensive or difficult. In that case, a sensitivity analysis may have to be performed on the whole company to determine the area or areas that do have a good potential for cost reduction. The procedure is the same whether the analysis is performed on the company or on a single department or product of the company.

Example: Palmer and Company makes furniture with annual sales of $10 million. Their operating expenses were as follows:

Sales	$1,000,000
G&A	100,000
Facilities	500,000
Labor	5,000,000
Materials	3,000,000
Total	$9,600,000

This gives it a 4% profit rate, extremely low for the industry. The obvious target for cost reduction is the cost of labor. Unfortunately, the furniture production can not be automated, except for some minor operations. As a result, very large labor cost reductions can not be made.

The company would like a profit of 25%. The profit of 4% translates into $400,000. A profit of 25% is $2.5 million. The best that could be done with labor cost savings of 15% is $750,000. An additional $1.75 million saving is needed. Obviously this would have to come from materials and/or sales costs. Facilities and G&A are very unlikely sources for substantial savings. Based on their share of the total costs, one-quarter of the $1.75 million is needed from sales and three-quarters from materials. This means $437,500 from sales and $1,312,500 from materials. These represent a 44% reduction in both sales expense and cost of materials. Both of the goals are possible, but both may be difficult. Large savings in materials can be realized by using different grades of woods without seriously affecting the quality. Using designs that require less material and reducing the number of models are other possibilities. The largest saving in cost of sales would be in the advertising budget. With an established reputation, there is no need for expensive campaigns.

Example: The Palmer example is a simple one, with an obvious solution. Suppose the operating expenses after considerable effort was expended on cost reduction were:

Sales	$ 750,000
G&A	100,000
Facilities	500,000
Labor	4,950,000
Materials	2,500,000
Total	$8,800,000

At this point, the profit rate on $10 million sales is 12%, a considerable improvement on the previous 4%, but still not equal to the average level for the industry.

It has been established that the 44% savings in sales and materials can not be achieved. The only recourse is to do a sensitivity analysis on the labor expense to determine whether further reductions are possible. The labor costs are the largest expense, 56% of the total costs, and therefore offer the greatest potential for savings.

In the first go-around, only the factory labor had been considered. This time the analysis has a better chance of success if all labor, direct and indirect, are examined. The total labor expense is determined as:

Manufacturing	$3,400,000
Quality Assurance	100,000
Receiving	100,000
Shipping	200,000
Warehouse	100,000
Engineering	50,000
Supervision	600,000
Order Processing	30,000
Maintenance	100,000
Industrial Engineering	25,000
Production Control	25,000
Purchasing	70,000
Marketing	100,000
Industrial Relations	50,000
Total	$4,950,000

The company is no longer looking for 25% profit but is willing to settle for 18%, a 50% increase over the 12% rate they had attained. This requires a saving of only $600,000. By examining the list of labor costs, management finds that certain reductions are feasible. The cuts recommended were as follows:

12% of manufacturing	=	$408,000
20% of supervision	=	120,000
20% of shipping	=	40,000
25% of marketing	=	25,000
10% of purchasing	=	7,000
Total		$600,000

After this exercise, other economies were found possible on other expense lines.

These examples are simple ones. In most cases, the sensitivity analysis is likely to be more complicated. Attempting to solve a large and complex network is usually beyond the skills of staff analysts. For that reason, the recommended procedure is to reduce the problem to a simple form. As previously stated, one technique is to select the most expensive area. Then select the most expensive item or items in that area. Continue down to the lowest level necessary for simplification. Then work back up to the top level.

Cost accounting is, to some extent, a form of sensitivity analysis. It can provide a breakdown of all the costs chargeable to a product or a department. The effectiveness of cost accounting can be increased if costs are not averaged. Multiproduct companies often use an average direct labor cost for charging each product. Quite often the direct labor cost is quite different for different products. Averaging conceals the disparity in unit costs. Averaging is also a problem with other costs such as plant, materials, and the like.

Augmented and miscroscopic cost accounting can be important tools in a DCR program. Accountants should definitely be a part of the DCR team, especially since most certified public accountants have had training and experience in sensitivity analysis.

SUMMARY

A major requirement for efficient cost reduction is establishing the areas to be attacked. The first step is to select the most expensive or the most complex area of the business as the most likely subject for cost reduction. The area can then be broken down to subsets. One can readily establish which of these subsets is the most costly, and, on this basis, make the decision to apply cost reduction. If large production quantities are involved, even an inexpensive part, such as a rivet, can yield substantial savings.

In the selection of alternative areas for cost reduction, keep in mind the analyst's prejudices. If he is an engineer, for example, he will tend to examine the engineering area.

It is not possible to predict with any accuracy how much cost reduction can be bought with each dollar spent on cutting costs. Although cost reduction is usually used to improve the profit picture, there are special cases where an increase in costs may provide greater profits. For example, an increased marketing budget may bring in enough sales so that, without any increase in productivity, profits rise substantially. Also, higher productivity may overcome the cost of increasing the labor force or the wages.

REFERENCES

1. C. T. Horngren, "Introduction to Management Accounting," Prentice-Hall, Inc., New Jersey, 1978, pp. 361–362.
2. I. Dlugatch, "Methodology for Value Engineering," IEEE Transactions on Reliability, vol. R–22, no. 1, April, 1973, pp. 20–23.
3. Department of Defense Handbook H111, "Value Engineering," March 29, 1963.

CASE STUDY: The H. G. Wolf Co.

The H. G. Wolf Co. had annual sales of $1,000,000. Their operating expenses were as follows:

Sales	$100,000
G&A	50,000
Facilities	50,000
Production	750,000
Total	$950,000
Net profit	$ 50,000 or 5%

The marketing manager estimated that, if he had $200,000 to spend, he could double the sales volume. This would mean doubling production. Assuming production costs were already at the flat portion of their curve, production costs could only be reduced 10% through purchasing economies. The operating budget would then be:

Sales	$ 200,000
G&A	50,000
Facilities	75,000
Production	1,350,000
Total	$1,675,000
Net profit	$ 325,000 or 16.25%

This would be an impressive improvement for a relatively small increase in expense. The production manager, however, pointed out that this was only an estimate and, in the present state of the economy, it had a low probability of success. Furthermore, production costs were escalating, so that the profit margin on the future sales could rapidly vanish. The production manager suggested that the best strategy was to improve the profit on the current sales volume. For example, suppose he could reduce production costs by about 10%. Then the operating expenses would be:

Sales	$100,000
G&A	50,000
Facilities	50,000
Production	675,000
Total	$875,000
Net profit	$125,000 or 12.5%

This was close to the profit improvement estimated by the sales manager. The production manager pointed out that a 10% reduction in production costs was not an unreasonable goal, and there was a high probability of achieving it. The president, Mr. Wolf, liked the loud sound of $325,000 profit better than the soft whisper of $125,000, but he had a third alternative. An expert consultant in cost reduction claimed that he could achieve as much as a 50 percent reduction in production costs because of his fresh viewpoint, his better knowledge of the state-of-the-art, and his broader experience. The consultant's operating expense budget was:

Sales	$100,000
G&A	50,000
Facilities	50,000
Production	375,000
Total	$575,000
Net profit	$425,000 or 42.5%

Admittedly this is a very unlikely net, but it is the kind of story that consultants tell to justify their bills. In this case, the consultant could have readily asked for $100,000, thus reducing the net to $325,000, exactly the amount promised by the sales manager.

It is now a question of which of the three alternatives Mr. Wolf should select. It is easy to reject the production manager's suggestion, because the goal is too low. What is left is the choice between cost reduction and cost increase. Mr. Wolf, at this point, should ask the sales manager to buy market research to provide data to support his plan, the sales manager should ask the consultant to provide him with a plan detailing how the reduction in production costs could be achieved. Only when Mr. Wolf obtained quantitative data should he attempt to make a decision.

The first step is to select the most expensive area of the business. For the H. C. Wolf Co., production costs are 79 percent of the total operating expense making production the target area.

Wolf manufactures a line of switch boxes for new dwellings. Fifty percent of their output is the Model W5A Circuit Breaker Assembly. Of the other products, none exceed 10 percent of the volume. The percentages are as follows:

Model	% of Production Cost
W5A	50
W1	8
W2	5
W2A	7
W3	8
W4	10
W4A	6
W5	6

Attention could be concentrated on the W5A if maximum impact for minimum selection is the object. However, such an aimless approach is not likely to achieve any worthwhile results. A goal should be established to help to decide where to look for the required savings.

Assume the following cost ratios exist for the various components of a circuit breaker assembly:

$$C_5/C_1 = 0.1$$
$$C_4/C_T = 0.1$$
$$C_3/(C_1 + C_2) = 0.15$$
$$C_2/C_1 = 0.3$$
$$C_T = \text{Total cost of assembly}$$

The relation of individual costs to the total cost is established by placing the cost ratios in the formula for the total cost:

$$C_T = C_1 + C_2 + C_3 + C_4 + C_5$$

To solve for C_1, for example, substitutions are made for C_2, C_3, C_4, and C_5 with their equivalents in terms of C_1. This yields

$$C_1 = 0.9C_T/1.595 = 0.564C_T$$

By this method it is determined that:

Cost	% of Total Cost
C_1	56.4
C_2	16.9
C_3	11.1
C_4	10.0
C_5	5.6

Based on these figures, a 20% cost reduction can be obtained either by a 40% saving on C_1 or an 18.9% saving on the sum of C_1, C_2, C_3, and C_4. The second alternative appears to be the best choice, because it requires the smallest and most easily achieved saving in each item attacked. This analysis proved to Mr. Wolf that the best plan was to ask the production manager to attempt a 20 percent reduction in production costs. Both the sales manager's and the consultant's plans were rejected.

CHAPTER 5

COST ANALYSIS AND CONTROL FOR DCR

Basic to the achievement of profit goals is an understanding of the true costs of every phase of a business undertaking. Cost analysis is a necessary activity before any cost reduction program can be initiated. The purpose of this chapter is not to restate the techniques currently in use but to point up the modifications of such analyses as required for DCR.

The same approach is used in the treatment of cost control. The basic control process involves:

1. Establishing standards representing desired performance.
2. Measuring performance against these standards.
3. Correcting deviations from the standards.

ANALYSIS PROCEDURES (1)

The steps to be followed in cost analysis are:

1. Select a measure that is representative of the activity being analyzed. This may be direct labor hours, tons or yards produced, orders processed, and the like.
2. Determine the actual dollars spent on any and all other company areas that can be charged to the activity being analyzed. An example would be the cost of the industrial relations chargeable to the production of the XYZ model.

At this point, the DCR program must depart from the conventional. The purpose of cost analysis, up to now, has been to determine which of the costs are fixed and which are variable. The reason for this determination is that only variable or a variable portion of costs were believed to be reducible.

All costs are classified on the basis of how they are affected by changes in volume of the item being costed. *Fixed costs* are those that remain constant, regardless of the business volume, such as rent, insurance, depreciation, and property taxes. *Variable costs* vary directly with volume. Examples of variable costs are sales commissions, materials, and production labor. In each of these there is a direct relationship between the costs and the increase or decrease in volume of operations. Also, such costs are not incurred when the plant or facility is opened but at the start of the particular production run or at the time the product is sold. *Mixed costs* have characteristics of both fixed and variable costs. They may take two possible forms:

1. Maintenance costs increasing in steps as the labor force is increased, thus, staying at a given level for a range of activity only.
2. Some types of production having a fixed base and increases as the volume increases.

Most costs are mixed costs, since rarely are costs fixed indefinitely, and some variables have fixed costs, such as scrap in materials.

Fixed costs are often called *burden costs* and are rarely treated as controllable. Therein lies our quarrel with this concept.

Classifying costs as fixed gives managers tunnel-vision.

Their concern with the "variable" costs blinds them to the more productive possibilities with many of the "fixed" costs.

Cost analysis is aided by forming a mathematical model of the activity. Stating the cost relations in an equation clears away any fuzziness that may exist in the mind of the analyst regarding these relations. One form, called a *policy model,* is useful when analyzing the costs for individual products in a multi-product company.

Example: The rules set down for the development of a policy model are:

1. Labor and material are direct costs.
2. All other costs are lumped together and treated as indirect costs.
3. Each product's indirect costs are some percentage of the total company indirect costs. This is usually called the overhead rate. It is computed by dividing the total company indirect costs by the total direct labor cost of all products.

For the purpose of the product cost formula, let:
DP = Direct labor cost for the product.
D = Direct labor cost for the company.
M = Material cost for the product.
B = Total company overhead.
R = Overhead rate = B/D.
C = Total product cost.
C = $DP(1 + R) + M$.

A machine shop project has the following costs:
DP = \$10,000 project direct labor cost.
D = \$500,000 company direct labor cost.
B = \$475,000 company overhead.
M = \$2,000 material cost.
R = B/D = 475,000/500,000 = 0.95.
C = $DP(1 + R) + M$ = 10,000(1 + 0.95) + 2,000 = \$21,500.

Example: The Allentyne Company was tracking the costs on its Model 3116 unit for the first six months of the year. Table 5.1 presents the data collected.

The first three months showed a gradual reduction in the unit costs and a constant direct labor unit cost of \$5. In April, both the total unit cost and the direct labor unit cost began to rise. In June, the total unit cost had increased 9.5% over the March rate—the direct labor cost, 18%.

The variable costs were direct labor, materials, and power. Both of the latter represented too small a percentage of the total

TABLE 5.1   COST ANALYSIS FOR MODEL 3116

	Jan.	Feb.	March	April	May	June
Volume in units	10,000	12,000	15,000	15,100	15,200	15,300
Direct labor	\$ 50,000	\$ 60,000	\$ 75,000	\$ 80,000	\$ 85,000	\$ 90,000
Materials	5,000	6,000	7,800	8,000	8,500	9,000
Plant	60,000	60,000	60,000	60,000	60,000	60,000
Power	2,500	3,000	3,500	4,000	4,500	5,000
G&A	10,500	11,000	11,500	11,500	12,000	12,000
Total costs	128,000	140,000	157,800	163,500	170,000	176,000
Unit cost	12.8	11.4	10.5	10.8	11.1	11.5
Unit direct labor	\$ 5.0	\$ 5.0	\$ 5.0	\$ 5.3	\$ 5.6	\$ 5.9

TABLE 5.2   MODEL 3116 COSTS BEFORE AND AFTER CORRECTION

	June	Percent	July	Percent
Volume in units	15,300	—	15,500	—
Direct labor	$ 90,000	51.1	$ 77,500	48.2
Materials	9,000	5.1	7,750	4.8
Plant	60,000	34.2	60,000	37.2
Power	5,000	2.8	3,875	2.4
G&A	12,000	6.8	12,000	7.4
Total	176,000		161,125	
Unit cost	11.5		10.3	
Unit direct labor	$ 5.9		$ 5.0	

cost to offer any potential for savings. Therefore, the industrial engineers directed all their efforts at reducing direct labor costs. In the process the industrial engineers reduced material and energy waste in addition. The result of the improvements for the month of July is shown in Table 5.2.

The unit cost was below the March figure and the direct labor cost was the same as in the first three months.

However, the earnings statement for the first quarter showed that Model 3116 was not profitable, even at the $10.5 unit cost. Obviously, the second quarter loss was even larger. Returning the cost to that of the first quarter, merely, reduced the loss and did nothing for the profitability.

The solution is obvious. The "fixed" cost, plant, is 37% of the total cost. Plant costs must be attacked. Certified public accountants are familiar with capital expenditure analysis.

CAPITAL EXPENDITURE ANALYSIS (CEA) (2)

Capital expenditure analysis (CEA) is an analysis of capital spending. Capital expenditures are, of course, fixed or non-current assets. Normally such an analysis would involve an estimate or forecast of future benefits. However, it can readilybe applied to a current situation, such as in the Allentyne example.

The forecast of future benefits can be obtained by such techniques as discounted cash flow rate of return, simulation, risk analysis, and network analysis. For DCR, sensitivity analysis is the recommended method.

Example: Referring to the Allentyne example, a unit cost of $7 is needed to give a 28.5% profit. There are only two fixed costs in this case, plant and G&A, and only plant has any real potential for savings. Allentyne owns the building and always buys new machines. Machines are replaced every 10 years. Because of a poor cash flow, Allentyne borrows heavily both for operating expenses and for capital investment. As a result, Model 3116 has had the following allocated for its share of plant costs:

Debt	$20,000
Machines	30,000
Facility	10,000
Total	$60,000

To cut the unit cost from $10.30 to $7 means a 32% reduction. This would require cutting $51,560 from the costs. The plant costs total only $60,000. This would have to be cut 85%, and this appears to be impossible. A 50% saving may be more reasonable and would result in an $8.45 unit cost and a 6.5% profit.

Any profit is better than a loss and the vice president–finances was asked to look into the matter. His solution was to sell the building and machines on a lease-back arrangement. The proceeds of the sale reduced the debt substantially. The $40,000 spent on capital equipment and the building was replaced by much lower lease payments. The 50% goal saving in fixed costs was readily achieved.

COSTING LABOR CONTRACTS (6)

The discounted cash flow technique is often used to analyze capital expenditures. Labor contracts also involve long-term commitments and varying patterns of cash flow. It is suggested, therefore, that labor contracts should be treated as a capital expenditure and analyzed similarly.

A common practice in labor negotiations is to evaluate contract proposals by comparing their costs-per-hour effects. This approach usually bases its conclusions on historical data. Actually it should be based on the labor input of future company activities and on the interrelationships between labor costs and other aspects of the firm's operations. The factors to be considered include effect of direct wage increase on fringe benefit costs, cost-of-living adjustments, compensation for time not worked, overtime premiums, and shift differentials.

The discounted cash flow method is recommended for evaluating labor contract proposals. Since this requires the skills of a CPA, we shall not attempt to detail the method here.

RETURN-ON-INVESTMENT ANALYSIS

Appropriate to the discussion of capital expenditure analysis is examination of return-on-investment analysis. Return-on-investment refers to the ratio of earnings to investment of capital. In the conventional form its calculation is based on the gross value of plant and working capital. This form of analysis has been introduced in the Profitability Index. But for DCR, capital assets are replaced with net worth or that portion of the net worth assigned to a particular product or department or division. This example demonstrates the difference:

Example: The Smith and Dale Company annual report yielded the following data.

Assets		
Cash	$ 2,050,000	
Receivables	3,500,000	
Inventories	2,000,000	
Deferred taxes	1,000,000	
Land & building	1,500,000	
Capital equipment	1,500,000	
Total		$11,550,000
Liabilities		
Debt	$ 1,170,000	
Payables	1,190,000	
Accrued expenses	1,000,000	
Income taxes	1,500,000	
Retirement benefits	2,000,000	
Total		$ 6,860,000
Net worth		$ 4,690,000
Sales		$ 8,900,000
Operating costs	$ 5,000,000	
Cost of sales	2,000,000	
Total		$ 7,000,000
Net		$ 1,900,000
Profit rate		21.3%

In the conventional method, investment would include:

Facility cost	$ 1,500,000
Capital equipment	1,500,000
Cost of capital	1,700,000
Operating costs	5,000,000
Cost of sales	2,000,000
Total investment	$11,170,000

Return-on-investment (ROI) = Profit/Investment
$$= 1,900,000/11,170,000$$
$$= 17.0\%$$

In the DCR program, this computation is

$$\text{Profit/Net Worth} = 1,900,000/4,690,000$$
$$= 40.5\%$$

The difference is due to the conventional calculation including operating costs in the investment. Since the profit already includes operating costs in its computation, these costs are not properly included in the investment. Operating costs and cost of sales normally are obtained as revenue and are not actual capital investments in the company.

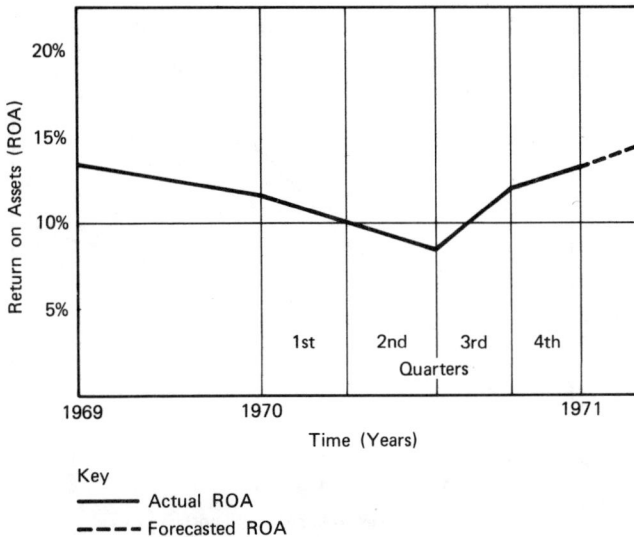

Key

―――― Actual ROA

▬ ▬ ▬ Forecasted ROA

Figure 11   Chart for Monitoring Return on Assets

At this point, another rate of return measure that is very similar to the ROI used for DCR should be mentioned. The Dupont Company pioneered the use of Return on Invested Assets (ROA). ROA is determined by multiplying profit (as a percent of sales) by sales (as a percent of investment). The investment allocated to produce the sales volume is used. This includes such items as cash, receivables, inventories, equipment, land and plant. The investment is the gross investment without deducting depreciation. Using goal ROA profitability, the ROA can be tracked as in Figure 11.

BREAK-EVEN ANALYSIS (3)

The return-on-investment analysis can be used in conjunction with a break-even analysis to determine the need for a cost reduction program. The *break-even point* is that point of the organization's capacity at which operations pass from profits to losses or vice versa. This is not a fixed point, since it will vary with management decisions, product price changes, and operating efficiency. The break-even point must be accurately defined, if good control is to be maintained over company profits. Figure 12 depicts a linear break-even analysis chart. This is the simplest form of this type of analysis. It is linear, because all plots are

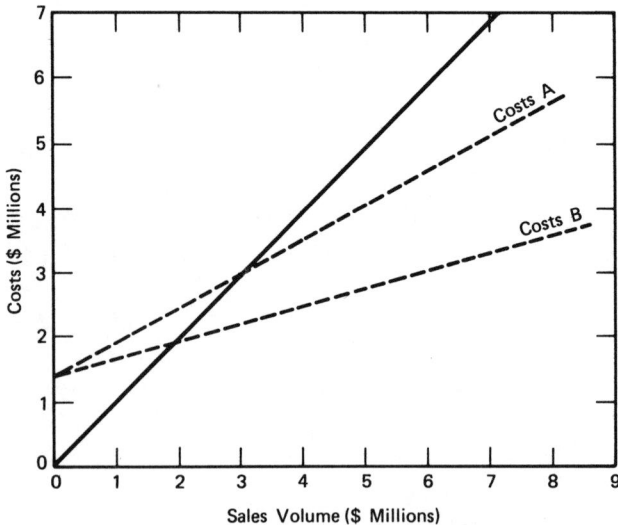

Figure 12   Linear Breakeven Analysis

straight lines and because the costs are directly proportional to the volume.

The solid line is a plot of all the break-even conditions. The dotted lines are the plots of cost of producing a particular volume. Where any particular cost line crosses the solid line is the break-even point for that level of costs. For example, line A crosses the solid line at $3 million sales and $3 million costs. The dotted line represents the variable costs only (they vary with volume). When the dotted line crosses the vertical scale (at $1.35 million) it marks the fixed costs. The fixed costs are the same at any level of output. Thus the dotted line is giving the sum of the fixed and variable costs. Note that this scheme permits a separation of costs so that an estimate can be made of the relative importance of the variable and fixed costs.

For example, line A tells us that, with zero output, we have $1.35 million in costs. At $3 million sales, the total costs are $3 million. Since the fixed costs are $1.35 million, the variable costs are the difference between the total and fixed expenses or $1.65 million.

The separation between the dotted line and the solid line is a measure of the profitability. It is sometimes called the *profit path*.

There are several ways to use the break-even analysis. For a start-up, this analysis, using a return-on-investment analysis as a guide, would determine that line A will never provide sufficient profit. The graphic representation permitted an analysis based on a limited number of calculations.

For example, it takes only two points to define a straight line. In this case, it is simple to establish the costs at zero output and the total costs at the break-even point for a relatively low level of volume. The analyst can readily project a cost line that would give an acceptable profit. Line B is such a line. The indication is that a cost reduction program is needed. Note that this has been established *before production has begun.*

The break-even analysis can be used to help in decisions about alternative options in sales, distribution, and products. In Figure 12, lines A and B could stand for two methods of distribution or for two different products. Line B would be the more profitable choice.

Some cautions on the use of the break-even analysis are necessary. The break-even model is a conceptual tool for estimating revenue. It is useful only over relatively short ranges of sales volume, because of the assumption of a linear relationship. There is no way of accurately predicting prices, demand, and costs beyond the immediate future. Therefore, the model should be used only as a guide for decision making and not as the determining factor.

INCREMENTAL ANALYSIS

The break-even analysis deals only with total costs and revenues. This is fine for a start-up situation but often is unsatisfactory for a going operation. It may be more helpful to know the costs for one additional unit. If that unit can be sold at a profit, it should be produced. *Incremental analysis* is useful in this kind of situation. Incremental means relating to a minute increase in quantity.

Figure 13 illustrates the measurement of the increments of cost and quantity of output. Q_T is the volume produced currently and Q_i is the incremental quantity. C_T is the cost of producing Q_T, and C_i is the incremental cost of producing Q_i. In the figure, we find $C_T = \$37,000$, $C_i = \$3,000$, $C_T + C_i = \$40,000$. $Q_T = 20,000$ units, and $Q_i = 3,000$ units. $Q_T + Q_i = 23,000$ units. The cost of producing 3,000 more units is $1 per unit. Note that the unit cost for producing 20,000 units is only 54 cents. The manager must now decide whether he can make an adequate profit at a one dollar unit cost. A break-even chart can be plotted (see Figure 12) using incremental costs and incremental sales volume. Figure 13 shows a straight line and, thus, would not yield a break-even point. Incremental analysis of a nonlinear relationship between costs and volume can give a break-even point.

A nonlinear break-even analysis might look like Figure 14. The shape of the cost curve may be due to any number of reasons, changes in pay rates, material shortages, inflation, and the like. There are two break-even points.

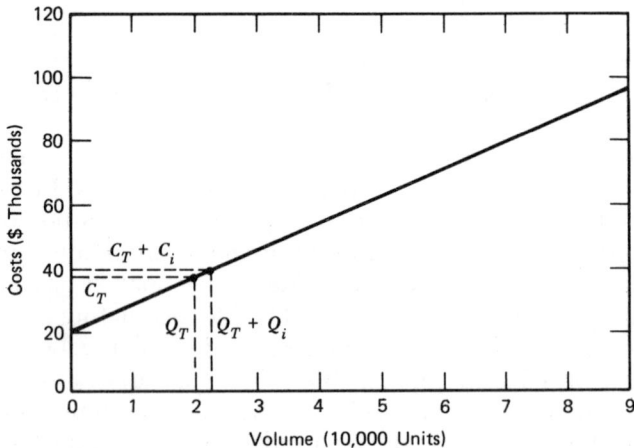

Figure 13   Incremental Cost Measurement

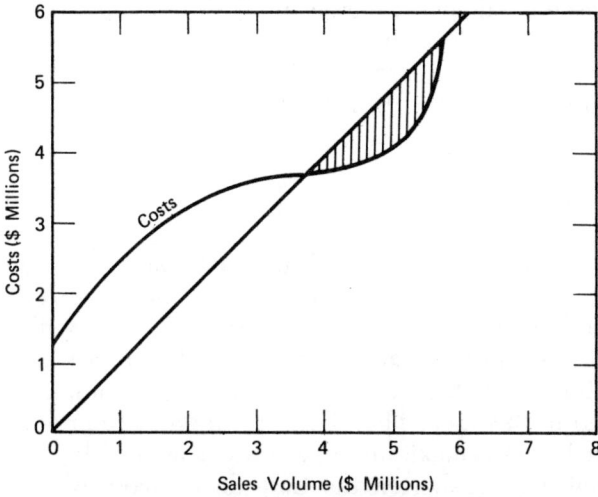

Figure 14   Nonlinear Breakeven Analysis

The profit is the cross-hatched area between the two curves and between the two break-even points. The profit that is of interest is the maximum possible value and it occurs at the maximum difference between the curves. In attempting an incremental break-even analysis, it is the incremental costs and incremental revenues for the cross-hatched area that is needed. Figure 15 shows a typical incremental break-even analysis.

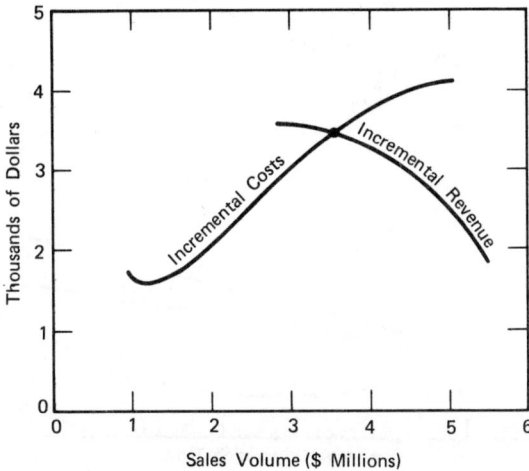

Figure 15   Incremental Breakeven Analysis

Here incremental cost is increasing with the volume, and the revenue is decreasing. Thus, the profit is increasing as the volume is decreasing. That is, any incremental increase in quantity beyond the break-even point will result in lowered profits.

MANPOWER COSTS

Industrial engineers are fairly skillful at analyzing and reducing direct labor costs. Therefore, the discussion of manpower costs will be limited to problems of time-cost. The main concern is with the time to complete tasks and the manpower to complete a task within a given time. The bounds on this cost will determine how much reduction can be obtained in this area. The efficiency of the worker and machine is not a factor because maximum efficiency is assumed.

The usual way to shorten the time for delivery is to increase the labor force. However, the costs involved in the increase in manpower is not a simple relationship. A time-cost analysis is necessary. Figure 16 is an example of such an analysis.

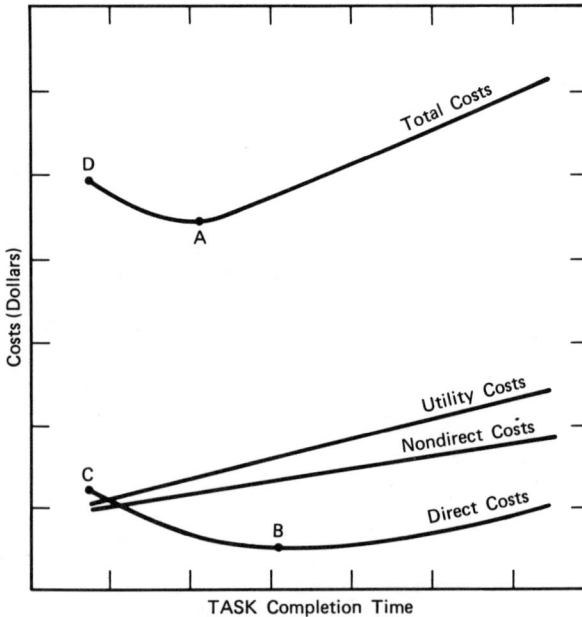

Figure 16   Time-Cost Analysis

Nondirect costs are assumed to increase linearly with time. *Utility costs* is a quantification of the penalty for not accomplishing the job at the earliest possible time. It, too, is shown as increasing linearly with time. The utility cost may be outage costs or loss-of-profit-opportunities (due to assignment of manpower to this project). The direct costs curve is not linear for many reasons such as overtime pay, materials cost, etc. Point C is the 'crash' point. That is, the job is performed on a crash basis with a large concentration of manpower so that a high labor cost is carried for only a short period.

Point B is the optimum point, because the direct costs are minimized. The longer the project takes, the less people are needed, but, obviously, there is some minimum number below which it is not possible to go. Very likely, the minimum number would be used at B. Thereafter, the costs increase, because the same number of men may be working on the project over an increasing length of time.

The total costs curve is the sum of all the three costs below. Now, there is a new and final optimum point, A, occurring somewhat earlier than B.

A chart, such as Figure 17, can be employed in conjunction with running cost data to measure how close the project is operating to the optimum point.

Deviations in this case may be normal if, for example, minimum cost

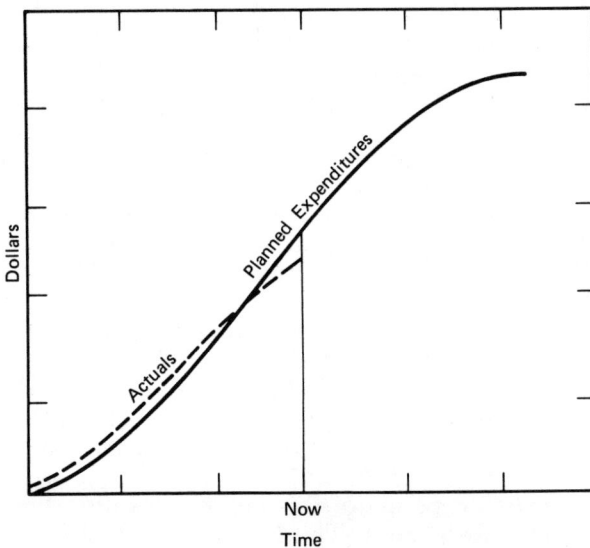

Figure 17 Time-Cost Control Chart

is less important than early delivery. However, it is possible to verify that additional funds can not obtain earlier delivery than is expected. That is, total costs greater than those at D in Figure 16 will not complete the job in less time.

In carrying out the control of job costs, it is helpful for the manager to plot actual against planned expenditures (obtained from Figure 16). He would maintain a chart like that of Figure 17 to compare the expenditures with the budget for the project. Such a chart does not give the reason for over-runs or under-runs, and the manager must seek other data for the explanation before taking action.

For the purposes of DCR, time-cost analysis is important to define the limitations on manpower costs. If this cost cannot be cut because of delivery requirements, then savings must be sought elsewhere.

Example: Two painters and one helper are redecorating an office building. It is estimated the job will take 20 working days and, at $20 per day for painters and $12 per day for the helper, will cost a total of $1040. If only one painter is used, the job will take 40 days, but the helper is still needed, making the labor cost, $1280, thus costing more than when three men are employed. The minimum cost of this task is $1040 and the activity duration at minimum cost is 20 days.

One can test other arrangements to reduce the activity duration. One possibility is having the three men work overtime every day to finish in 18 days, but this will cost (due to overtime rates) $1092. Another possibility is to add a third painter, but this requires an additional helper so that even if the time to complete the work is reduced to $13\frac{1}{3}$ days, the labor cost is $1120. Finally, a fourth painter could be added, but they can not work as efficiently because of large interference with the business of the tenants if all the painting was concentrated in one office. Separating into teams is not too helpful because of the need to support two locations with materials and supervision. As a result, with four painters and two helpers, the job would take 11 days at a cost of $1144.

Of the five possible ways of performing the activity, the 40 day, 2 man solution can be dropped, since it offers no advantage in either time or cost, but the other four are all useful for determining the increased cost for speeding up the job. The relationship, for each solution, which exists between time to complete and activity cost is plotted in Figure 18.

The two extreme points of this curve are called the Normal point and the Crash point. The Normal point shows the time required to perform the activity at minimum cost. The Crash

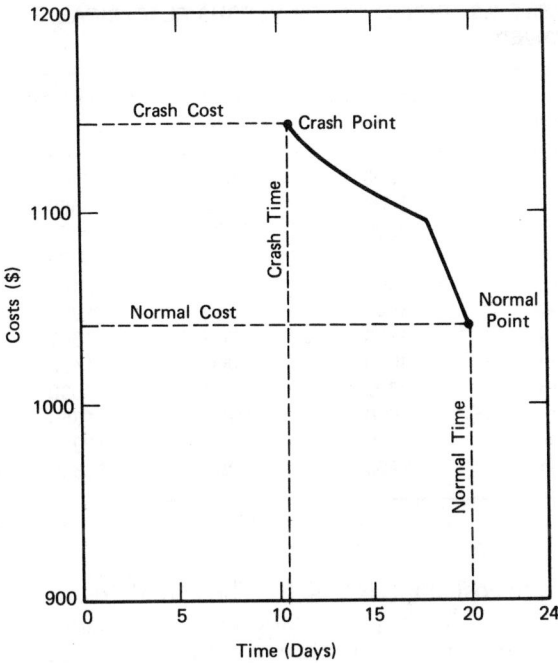

Figure 18   Activity Time/Cost Relationships

point shows the minimum time in which it is possible to perform the activity with the associated cost. The curve is useful for approximating the infinite variety of time and cost combinations that exist between the two extreme points if it is assumed that there is a straight line between the two points.

The *cost slope* of an activity is the cost of shortening the activity by one time unit. Thus, if an activity has a cost slope of $50 and is on the critical path, the project duration could be reduced by one day at an additional cost of $50. The cost slope is calculated from:

$$\text{Cost Slope} = \frac{\text{Crash Cost} - \text{Normal Cost}}{\text{Normal Time} - \text{Crash Time}}$$

In Figure 18, there are three separate cost slopes. They are computed as follows:

Time Reduction

20 to 18	($1092 − $1040)/(20 − 18) = $26
18 to 13⅓	($1120 − $1092)/(18 − 13⅓) = $6
13⅓ to 11	($1144 − $1120)/(13⅓ − 11) = $10.5

TABLE 5.3   DIRECT LABOR VERSUS ELECTRICAL POWER

Month	Direct Labor Hours	Power Cost	Recvg./Ship. Labor Cost
Jan.	5000	$2500	$2500
Feb.	5500	3000	2550
Mar.	6600	3100	3000
Apr.	6000	2500	3000
May	5200	2250	2400
June	4400	1950	1950
July	3500	2200	1500
Aug.	4000	2000	1450
Sept.	3800	2500	1500
Oct.	4000	2400	1550
Nov.	4800	2400	$2050
Dec.	3900	$2200	$1500

The average cost slope is $14.16. The calculated cost slopes for each activity enables a quick selection to be made of those activities on a network whose time duration can be reduced with the minimum increase of cost, since the lower the value of the cost slope, the lower the increase in cost for each time unit saved. There will be special cases where the general assumptions made above do not apply. It may not be possible to reduce the time of an activity at any price, or the normal time and crash time may be obtained by using two entirely different labor forces.

Example: Electrical power and receiving and shipping labor costs are to be analyzed for the Oxo Electronics Co. It has been determined that the total direct labor hours in the plant are a realistic measure of plant activity. The data to be analyzed are in Table 5.3.

A graph is plotted with direct labor hours on the horizontal scale and electrical power costs along the vertical scale (Figure 19).

The fixed electrical power cost is on the dollar scale where the line intersects the dollar costs scale. Fixed electrical power cost is $950. The variable cost is the slope of the line which is computed by dividing the cost of electrical power at any point on the line by the number of direct labor hours for that point. Variable cost is 62.5¢ per labor hour. This cost is used as a standard for electrical power that can be used to compare with each month's

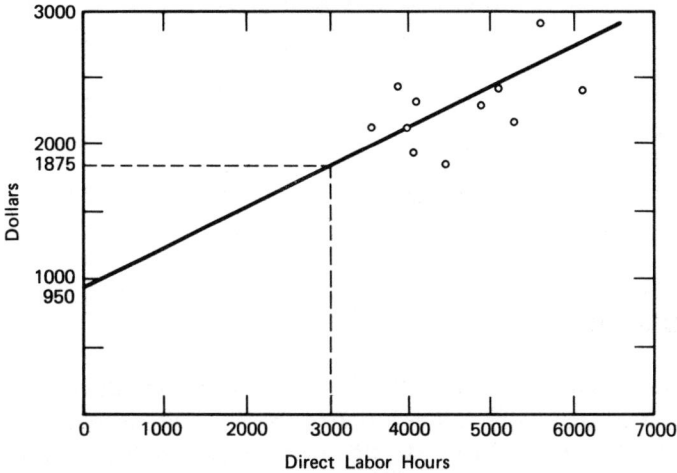

Figure 19   Monthly Power Costs

power cost as a control measure. If the power cost is higher, corrective action is indicated.

Figure 20 is a graph plotted for monthly labor costs. Considering only the plotted points, one might conclude that a linear relationship exists between this cost and activity. This is not true.

A given crew size is adequate up to a certain level of activity. Beyond that activity, additional manpower must be added. Therefore, the cost rises in steps. Table 5.4 shows the stepped mixed costs.

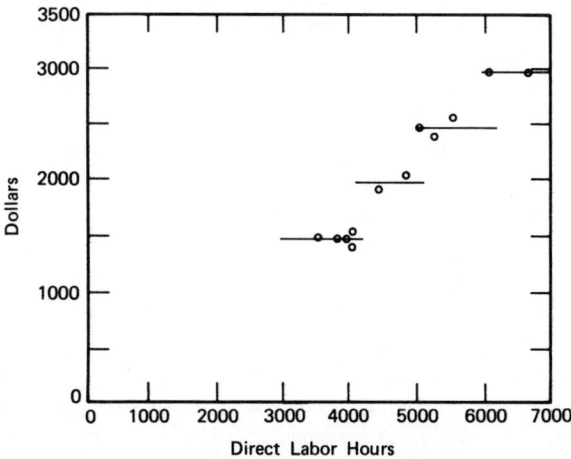

Figure 20   Monthly Labor Costs

TABLE 5.4   STEPPED MIXED LABOR COSTS

Direct Labor Hours	Cost
3000 to 4000	$1500
4001 to 5000	2000
5001 to 6000	2500
6001 to 7000	$3000

COST CONTROL

It is not sufficient for profitability to merely cut costs. It is also important to control costs upon completion of the reduction program in order to maintain the profitability. In this section, we shall examine only a few of the control measures open to the manager, and the effect of DCR on these controls.

Budgets

Figure 17 is an example of a *variable budget.* In this case, the funds allotted to that operation vary from month to month, because of different numbers of workers assigned to the operation as it passes through various phases such as planning, engineering, production, etc. In other operations, the budget may vary because of seasonal markets. *Fixed budgets* are more usual for managerial actions that will not yield results within a given accounting period. DCR is effective and necessary before the initiation of a fixed budget. DCR is effective any time with a variable budget.

A common over-all control device is a summary of budgets, a summary of all the individual budgets of the organization. This summary can contain reports from sales, production, engineering, etc. the appropriate outputs or forecasts to expenditures. Each department uses its forecasts to prepare expenditure budgets along with statements of costs, output, and requirements. With the summary, the budget maker develops a balance sheet and a statement of profit and loss to accompany the final budget. The three documents permit top management to measure over-all performance.

The report accompanying the budget summary should have, at the least, calculated variances and explanations of the variances. This is necessary, because the executive who receives the summary and is responsible for the control, is too far removed from the source of the information to be aware of the cause for the deviations.

The profit and loss statement is an extremely important over-all control tool as well as a DCR tool. It is a good summary of the operations. It is effective in defining the contribution of each company subdivision to the objective of profitability.

When a department prepares a profit and loss statement, it is as though the department were an independent entity instead of a component of a large organization. For a DCR program, it is not essential that the unit produce and market a product in order to use profit and loss control, nor does it need to sell its services to other departments. This is because sensitivity analysis can be used to determine precisely the *sensitivity index* for the department's costs. For example, suppose it is determined that the engineering service department has a sensitivity index of 0.0001. This would mean that an increase of $10,000 in the costs of the department will increase the total operating costs, one dollar. This is determined by multiplying the index by the increase in department costs. In lieu of a profit or loss, the department can show an increase or decrease in its cost referenced by the sensitivity index to the total operating costs.

The important over-all DCR cost control tool is the profitability index (see Chapter 2). The budgets for the individual departments will each have a profitability index as well as the over-all budget. In essence we have a special DCR budget organization like that of Table 5.5.

The company budget integrates only producing department budgets. Nonproducing departments usually serve more than one producing department. They need to supply as many budgets as there are producing departments. Therefore, there are the same number of

TABLE 5.5 DCR BUDGET ORGANIZATION

	Requirements
Company Budget	Statement of Earnings
	Balance Sheet
	Profitability Index
Producing Department Budget	Statement of Earnings
	Profitability Index
Nonproducing Department Budget	Cost Analysis
	Sensitivity Index

TABLE 5.6   E. V. SMITH & CO. BUDGET DATA

E. V. Smith & Co.	
Revenues	$13,005,000
Expenses	10,120,000
Net	$ 2,885,000
Assets	$ 6,350,000
Liabilities	2,490,000
Net Worth	$ 3,860,000
Profitability Index	0.74
Computer Peripheral Division	
Revenues	$ 6,190,000
Expenses	5,000,000
Net	$ 1,190,000
Profitability Index	0.64
Computer Peripheral Engineering Department	
Budget Costs	$ 1,000,000
Sensitivity Index	0.2

cost analyses and sensitivity indices, since the costs referenced are the costs of the producing department receiving the budget.

Example: The calculations involved in generating the data of Table 5.6 are:

$$\text{Company PI} = \text{Company Profit/Net Worth}$$
$$= \$2,885,000/\$3,860,000 = 0.74$$

$$\text{Computer Peripheral Div. PI} = \frac{\text{Div. Profit}}{\text{Div. Share of Net Worth}}$$

Without better information we have to compute the Division's share of net worth on the basis of its share of total expenses:

$$\text{Division net worth} = \text{Company net worth} \times \frac{\text{Div. Expense}}{\text{Comp. Expense}}$$
$$= \$3,860,000 \times \$5,000,000/\$10,120,000$$
$$= \$3,860,000 \times 0.48 = \$1,852,800$$

$$\text{Division PI} = \$1,190,000/\$1,852,800 = \$0.64$$

$$\text{Engrg. Dept. Sensitivity Index} = \frac{\text{Dept. Costs}}{\text{Div. Costs}}$$
$$= \$1,000,000/\$5,000,000$$
$$= 0.2$$

Example: The plating department of a company published the following statement of earnings:

Revenues	$240,000
Expenses	200,000
Net	$ 40,000

The company financial data was:

Revenue	$1,000,000
Expenses	800,000
Net	$ 200,000
Assets	2,000,000
Liabilities	1,000,000
Net worth	$1,000,000

The PI for the company is $200,000/$1,000,000 = 0.2. The PI for the plating department is $40,000/$240,000 = 0.16. The investment in the plating department is $240,000. The plating maintenance department has budget costs of $25,000. Its sensitivity index is $25,000/$200,000 = 0.125. If the maintenance budget is cut 10%, the effect on the plating department costs is 10% of 12.5% or a reduction of 1.25%.

Engineering Budgets (7)

Engineering budgets are normally the estimated costs of operation for a specific period. It is a major problem for management to monitor the level of spending effort. If the budget was properly prepared and the engineering effort efficiently applied, the task or tasks would be completed within the scheduled time and with little or no variance from the budget dollars. However, an operational reporting system is necessary to ensure achieving these goals. The reporting system will reveal the existence of significant variances (over or under), indicating mismanagement of the activities. An underrun is just as bad as an overrun. Both mean the program goals are not being achieved in an orderly manner. The reporting alone can not be a control. A simulation is needed to establish levels of the future spending needed to bring performance back within the acceptable ranges of tolerance.

Stated simply, funds are fixed so that, if too much is spent at one point because of some difficulty, there may not be enough money to complete the project. It is usually difficult to obtain additional funds, especially if the overrun is due to unanticipated problems. Providers of funds are apt to be skeptical of the ultimate success of any program running into financial difficulties.

A technique for monitoring the level of spending effort for fixed budgets is to modify the spending targets for each remaining report period based on the unspent amount of the project budget. Using this technique over the entire period of the project schedule permits management to maneuver the level of spending effort based on past experience and knowledge of the remaining funds and time. Suppose the project has a budget of $144,000 to be used in equal amounts in each of 12 reporting periods. The level of spending planned would be $144,000/12 or $12,000 per period. At the end of each period, a new target is computed for the remaining periods by dividing the balance of the funds by the number of remaining periods. This is illustrated by Table 5.7.

This table is developed in the following manner:

Reporting period 0: the start of the project budget. The only entries are the project funding of $144,000 and the number of remaining periods.

First reporting period: target amount is computed by dividing column five by column six (of the previous reporting period), or $144,000/12. The third column is the actual funds expended during this period or $9,900. The fourth column is the difference between the

TABLE 5.7   LEVEL OF SPENDING COMPUTATIONS

Reporting Period	Target	Actual	Variance	Funds Balance	Periods Remaining
0	—	—	—	$144,000	12
1	$12,000	$ 9,900	$(2,100)	134,100	11
2	12,190	14,000	1,810	120,000	10
3	12,000	20,000	8,000	100,000	9
4	11,111	21,000	9,889	79,000	8
5	9,875	9,000	(875)	70,000	7
6	10,000	10,000	0	60,000	6
7	10,000	15,000	5,000	45,000	5
8	9,000	11,000	2,000	34,000	4
9	8,500	7,000	(1,500)	27,000	3
10	9,000	8,000	(1,000)	19,000	2
11	9,500	9,500	0	9,500	1
12	$ 9,500	$ 9,000	$ (500)	$ 500	0

period's target and the actual—$12,000 minus $9,900 or $2,100 under target. This is shown in parentheses to indicate a negative variance. The funds balance, of course, is the balance of the previous period, $144,000, less the actual funds expended or $134,100. The last column is the number of periods remaining, 11.

The remaining entries in Table 5.7 are computed in the same manner. The method illustrated does not correct the rate of expending funds, but it does inform management of trends. Management knows the minimum needed to complete the task and can act when this minimum is endangered.

Uniform spending in each of the reporting periods is extremely rare. Usually there is a swift buildup and a slow decline in spending as the effort moves through the various phases: acquiring data, studying requirements, design, development, and specification. As a result, the planned level of spending is not equal for each reporting period.

For the nonuniform level of spending budget, the method used is as follows:

Assume the dollar budget for a one year project is $118,000. It is necessary to develop an adjustment factor by which the targets planned for any specific period can be adjusted to take up the slack as the funds are expended. The factors are developed, beginning with the second period, because the variance of the preceding period is needed for the computation. Table 5.8 illustrates the computation of the adjustment factors.

Table 5.8 is computed in the following manner:

The numerator is the original planned target for the immediate reporting period. The denominator is the sum of all the remaining planned targets, beginning with the immediate reporting period. Thus, for the second period, the numerator is the planned target for that period, $8,000. The denominator is the sum of all the remaining planned targets, $112,000. The factor is $8,000/$112,000. The other factors are computed in the same fashion.

Table 5.9 is the new level of spending chart, using the adjustment factors of Table 5.8.

The funds balance at the beginning of the immediate reporting period is multiplied by the adjustment factor. The chart is developed in the following fashion:

For the second period, the planned target is $8,000. This is multiplied by the adjustment factor obtained from Table 5.6, 8/112, to obtain $8,071. The variance is now the difference between the adjusted target and the actual, $8,071 − $5,000 or $3,071. The balance is the difference between the balance of the preceding periods balance and

TABLE 5.8 FACTORS FOR ADJUSTMENTS

Periods	11	10	9	8	7	6	5	4	3	2	Factor
											Planned Targets Remaining
2	$ 8000										8/112
3	9000	$ 9000									9/104
4	10000	10000	$10000								10/95
5	11000	11000	11000	$11000							11/85
6	12000	12000	12000	12000	$12000						12/74
7	12000	12000	12000	12000	12000	$12000					12/62
8	12000	12000	12000	12000	12000	12000	$12000				12/50
9	11000	11000	11000	11000	11000	11000	11000	$11000			11/38
10	10000	10000	10000	10000	10000	10000	10000	10000	$10000		10/27
11	9000	9000	9000	9000	9000	9000	9000	9000	9000	$ 9000	9/17
12	8000	8000	8000	8000	8000	8000	8000	8000	8000	8000	8/8
	$112000	$104000	$95000	$85000	$74000	$62000	$50000	$38000	$27000	$17000	

TABLE 5.9 LEVEL OF SPENDING COMPUTATIONS

Period	Planned Target	Adjusted Target[a]	Actual	Variance	Funds Bal.	Per. Left
0	—	—	—	—	$118,000	12
1	$. 6,000	—	$ 5,000	$(1,000)	113,000	11
2	8,000	$ 8,071	5,000	(3,071)	108,000	10
3	9,000	9,355	5,000	(4,355)	103,000	9
4	10,000	10,842	8,000	(2,842)	95,000	8
5	11,000	12,294	10,000	(2,294)	85,000	7
6	12,000	13,783	18,500	4,717	66,500	6
7	12,000	12,872	13,000	128	53,500	5
8	12,000	12,840	12,000	(840)	41,500	4
9	11,000	12,013	13,000	987	27,500	3
10	10,000	10,148	11,000	852	16,500	2
11	9,000	8,735	8,000	(735)	8,500	1
12	$ 8,000	$ 8,500	$ 8,000	$ (500)	$ 500	0

[a] Adjustment factor × funds balance

the actual, $113,000 − $5,000 or $108,000. The remaining entries are computed in the same manner.

The second technique for engineering spending level control provides for the establishment of tolerance limits. Obviously, the range of tolerance can be quite large in the early stages of the project, since a small increment from each of the remaining periods will be sufficient to compensate for a very large variance in the first few periods. As the completion date comes closer, there is less room for correction, and the range of tolerance must become tighter. Figure 21 illustrates this.

It is unrealistic to assume that actual spending will equal targets in any given period. At the end of the budget period, the smaller ranges of tolerance mean management must be alerted much earlier whenever actuals lie outside the range of tolerance. Variances are usually very much larger during early periods, because these are the learning periods. In the last few periods, actuals lower than the negative tolerance require no management action, since this represents a possible surplus at the conclusion of the project.

Inventory Cost Control (3,4)

A firm's inventory includes not only completed products awaiting shipment to customers, but also the material for manufacturing the products, the manpower required for the operations, and the machines or other equipment in the plant. The problem common to all these

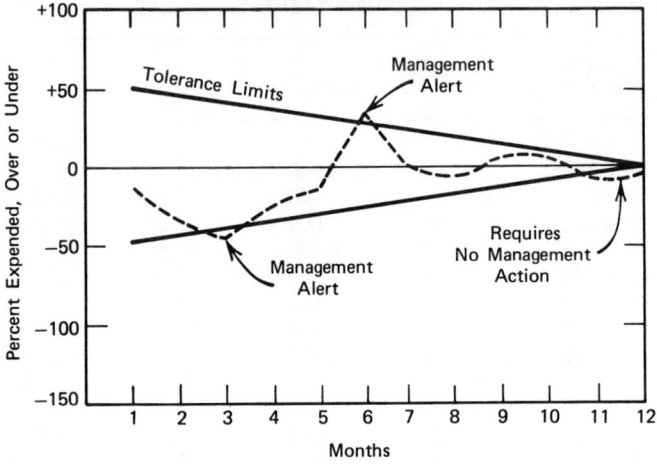

Figure 21   Research Spending Chart

items is that of minimizing the costs of maintaining the inventory while, simultaneously, fulfilling customer demands. The interest for DCR is that the cost standards can be optimized but cannot be arbitrarily reduced.

The inventory cost factors include:

Ordering Costs (OC). These are the clerical and administrative costs per order as well as the cost of receiving and stocking the goods. This cost is computed by

$$OC = \frac{\text{Quantity needed } (D) \times \text{Cost of placing order } (J)}{\text{Size of each order } (Q)}$$

It is assumed all orders are the same size.

Example: 10,000 cases are needed for 6 months production. It costs $10 to place an order and each order is for 1,000 cases.

$$OC = \frac{10,000 \times \$10}{1,000} = \$100$$

Carrying Costs (CC). These include interest not earned on money used for inventory, cost of space, obsolescence, taxes, and insurance. Carrying cost is computed by

CC = Half order size (Q/2) × Unit value (V)
$\qquad\qquad$ × Percent of value estimated carrying cost (E)

It is assumed that the order size is twice the average inventory.

Example: The cases have a unit value of $5, and it is estimated that the carrying cost is 10% of the unit value.

$$CC = 500 \times \$5 \times 0.1 = \$250$$

It is essential to determine the optimum inventory and order size to minimize costs. When trying to find the best inventory and ordering quantity, it is usually assumed that the demand for an item and the time for delivery of the orders are both known exactly. Also, it is assumed that the rate at which items are taken out of inventory is constant. The same number of units are used each day. These assumptions are not at all realistic, but they make it easy to derive a formula for computing the best order size. The formula can then be adjusted to reflect variations in the demand, delivery time, and the use rate.

The formula to be used is called the *Economic Order Quantity* (*EOQ*). The formula is developed by plotting curves for both ordering costs and carrying costs on the same chart. This is done in Figure 22.

The curves cross at point A, which means the carrying cost is exactly equal to the ordering cost or $CC = OC$. *EOQ* is that order size at which

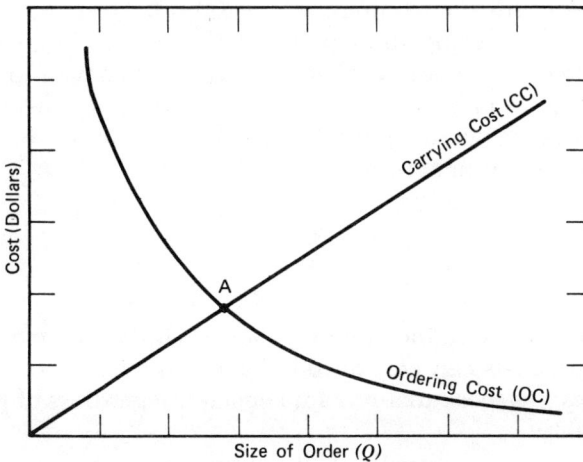

Figure 22   Carrying Cost versus Ordering Cost

the two curves cross and

$$EOQ = (2DJ/VE)^{\frac{1}{2}}$$

Example:

$$D = 500 \text{ units}$$
$$J = \$15$$
$$E = 15\%$$
$$V = \$10$$

$$EOQ = [(2 \times 500 \times 15)/(10 \times 0.15)]^{\frac{1}{2}} = 100 \text{ units}$$

Therefore, the lowest cost ordering scheme is 500/100 or 5 orders of 100 units each.

Suppose the demand was not constant. For example, $D = 500$ for 6 weeks and $D = 800$ for 4 weeks after that. Then, for the 6 week period (6 weeks/10 weeks = 0.6):

$$EOQ = [(2 \times 500 \times 15)/(10 \times 0.15 \times 0.6)]^{\frac{1}{2}} = 129$$

The six week ordering strategy = 500/129 = 3+
Likewise, for the last 4 week period:

$$EOQ = [(2 \times 800 \times 15)/(10 \times 0.15 \times 0.4)]^{\frac{1}{2}} = 200$$

The four week ordering strategy = 800/200 = 4

The six week ordering strategy is difficult to use (3+ orders of 129 units). The manager would probably modify this answer to arrive at 4 orders of 125 units or 3 orders of 167 units. His decision would depend on which strategy would keep the production lines from stopping because of a lack of materials.

SUMMARY

The costs can not be reduced unless they are fully understood. This is because some costs can be controlled and some can not.

Fixed costs are those that remain constant, regardless of production or sales volume.

Variable costs vary directly with volume.

Mixed costs combine the characteristics of fixed and variable costs.

At any given level of an organization, the manager has control over certain costs but no influence at all over other costs. Therefore, he has to learn to distinguish between controllable and noncontrollable costs. Then he can concentrate on reducing the controllable costs, and not waste time on cost factors he cannot influence.

Managers generally think of variable expenses as controllable and fixed expenses as noncontrollable. For this reason, they believe that variable expenses are susceptible to cost reduction and fixed expenses are irreducible. Actually, fixed costs can be made to behave like variable expenses. For example, the occupancy cost for a given size building can vary as much as 50% between different locations. Another illustration is maintenance. This is a fixed cost as long as a maintenance crew is on the payroll, but if the maintenance people are replaced with a contract to an outside maintenance organization, a variable maintenance cost results, and a sizable reduction in costs may be obtained.

If unit costs are considered, the fixed/variable definitions are altered. The fixed portion of the unit cost of a product varies inversely with the volume. The variable portion is fixed with volume. This means that a very large reduction in unit costs can be obtained from greater volume for an existing production unit. For example, the Joy Toy Company produced equal quantities of wagons and large rocking horses. The horse requires twice as much labor and space to manufacture as the wagon. Changing the product mix to produce twice as many wagons as horses increased productivity and thereby lowered the fixed unit costs of building and equipment. And the new product mix produced a higher profit.

Return-on-investment refers to the ratio of earnings to investment of capital. Its calculation is based on the gross value of plant and working capital. An asset produces net income until it is retired from use. Some companies base the calculation on fixed assets less depreciation, because the depreciation reserve represents a write-off of the initial investment and funds made available in this way are reinvested in other fixed assets or used as working capital.

In a return-on-investment analysis, curves such as those in Figures 23 and 24, are plotted for each product. Figure 23 shows the cost per unit of the Model K10A product of the Smith & Dale Co. Figure 24 plots the return-on-investment for the same product. It demonstrates the importance of this type of analysis to cost reduction programs. It is obvious that any cost reduction program attempted before the break-even point in production had been reached would be a waste of time.

Return-on-investment is calculated in the following manner:

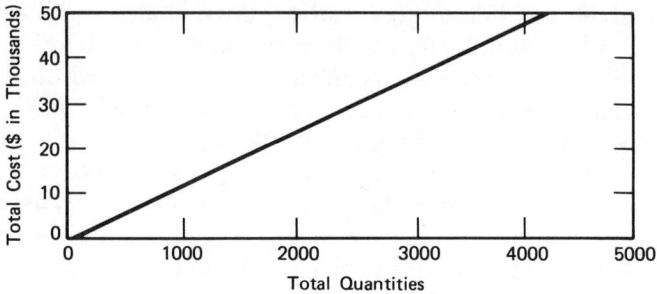

Figure 23   Unit Production Cost, Model K10A

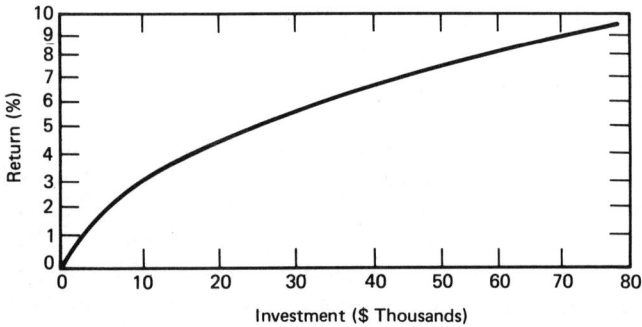

Figure 24   Return on Investment, Model K10A

Total investment in a product is the total capital investment, plus operating costs, plus cost of the capital.

$$\text{Return-on-Investment} = \frac{\text{Sales} \times \text{Earnings Percent}}{\text{Total Investment}}$$

Some general comments on cost analysis:

1. Be familiar with the operations. Wrong conclusions can be drawn from the data alone.
2. Analysis results depend heavily on the quality of the cost data. Do not lump together large, continuing items of cost.
3. Charge costs as close to the time of use as possible. When a three months' supply of an item is charged to a department at one time, the costs are distorted for all three months.
4. Plotting cost data against activity will point up wide deviations. Assuming the basic data are correct, one can more readily find where cost control needs to be applied.

5. When one or more plotted points fall well above the line, further and detailed study of those months can uncover poor operating practices that warrant correction. Conversely, points well below the line reveal a temporary method or practice that should become standard.
6. If plots of monthly data result in an ambiguous pattern, try plotting bimonthly data. A pattern may be revealed with less data.

It is important to control costs upon completion of the reduction program, if profitability is to be maintained. Budgets are one form of cost control. Company-wide control by budget could be a summary budget integrating the individual departmental budgets. All budgets should be accompanied by a balance sheet and a statement of profit and loss. The three documents permit top management to measure the overall performance. However, management needs calculated variances and explanations of the variances.

Engineering budgets are normally the estimated costs of operation for a specific period. For control of engineering budgets, a spending schedule is needed that modifies the spending target for each remaining period based on the unspent amount of the project budget.

Cost standards for control of inventory costs can be optimized but cannot be arbitrarily reduced. The problem is that of minimizing the costs of maintaining the inventory while, simultaneously, fulfilling customer demands. The clerical and administrative costs per order as well as the cost of receiving and stocking the goods is calculated by

$$\frac{\text{Quantity Needed} \times \text{Cost of Placing an Order}}{\text{Size of Each Order}}$$

The cost of carrying the inventory is computed by

Half the Order Size × Unit Cost × Carrying Cost (% of Unit Cost)

REFERENCES

1. L. M. Matthews, "Profit by Learning Cost Analysis," *Electronic Design*, no. 23, Nov. 8, 1967, pp. 96–218.
2. M. H. Abdelsamad and J. B. Sperry, "Capital Expenditure Analysis and the CPA's Responsibility," *Management Adviser*, May–June, 1974, pp. 39–45.
3. J. H. Donnelly Jr., et al., *"Fundamentals of Management,"* Business Publications, Austin, Texas, 1971, Chapter 15.
4. E. S. Buffa, *"Production-Inventory Systems: Planning and Control,"* Richard D. Irwin, Homewood, Il., 1968.

5. P. E. Torgersen and I. T. Weinstock, *"Management: An Integrated Approach,"* Prentice-Hall, New Jersey, 1972, Chapter 7.
6. M. H. Granof, "How To Cost Your Labor Contract," *The Bureau of National Affairs, Inc.,* Washington, D.C.
7. J. B. Edwards, "Monitoring the Level of Spending Effort for Lump-Sum Grants," *Management Adviser,* March–April, 1974, pp. 44–47.

CASE STUDY: THE GREASE PENCILS CORPORATION

The Nilsen family had been operating the Grease Pencils Corporation for some thirty years. They were producing marking pencils of many types and colors. The company was started when Gus Nilsen discovered a need for good quality, low priced crayons to be used by shipping clerks. Until then, such marking crayons had been either byproducts of wax producers and usually sold by toy stores. Thus, they were rarely made with man-sized dimensions and were frequently broken. Color quality was poor and nonuniform.

Nilsen was employed in the production of crayons and had developed a method of homogenizing carbon particles with wax and other ingredients resulting in a firmer and stronger crayon. In addition, in use, the crayons wrote with an oily mark that did not peel or skip. Nilsen crayons found a ready market and the users soon came to call the markers "grease pencils," because of the appearance of the writing done with them. Sales spiralled upward very quickly for the young company. As the word spread nationally about the Nilsen product, it saved time to talk to prospective customers about "grease pencils," and it was a simple transition for the company to change its name from Nilsen and Company to Grease Pencils Incorporated.

Despite the quick acceptance of the marking crayons, the market was too limited for the company to grow to any sizeable proportions. Gus Nilsen knew his own limitations. His experience was confined to crayons. He knew he would have to develop new products and new applications. Automation, particularly in addressing packages, was a real threat to the future of Grease Pencils Incorporated. Without any professional research assistance, Nilsen came up with a crayon with markings that could be wiped off any surface with a cloth. This product was needed badly by most government services for marking maps. Sales of this product were even more phenomenal than for the basic black marker. Soon there was a demand for other colors, not only for the map marker, but also for the grease pencils. An artist friend suggested an oil color crayon for a new technique he felt would catch on very quickly. Colors require a knowledge of physics and chemistry that were beyond the ability of Gus Nilsen.

To meet the need, Grease Pencils Inc. made its first investment in research and development. A chemist was hired and instructed to set up a laboratory which, at minimum cost, could develop the colors and the body for the new crayons. The chemist, Dr. Wilbur Clemens, requested a budget of $150,000 for the first year. This was to include salaries for himself and two laboratory technicians, some laboratory furnishings, and a considerable amount of supplies. Dr. Clemens promised he would have firm results by the end of the year and some additional ideas for new products to be developed in the succeeding years. The research budget was far more than Nilsen had anticipated, and he was somewhat reluctant to go ahead without some assurance that the rewards were worth the risk.

Nilsen and Clemens met to discuss the budget. First they examined the estimates available on the market potential. These varied from the optimistic forecasts of the artist to the more pessimistic ones of Nilsen's brother, George, who managed the sales department. They agreed finally on an average of all the estimates, a figure of $1,000,000 within three years of the introduction of the new product. In the light of this prediction, the $150,000 budget seemed to be too high. The company's status was not good enough to make any tax saving important enough to offset the erosion of the cash balance. Nilsen asked for a 50% reduction of the research budget and finally compromised on a figure of $90,000. Dr. Clemens pointed out that such austerity was based on a stretchout of the product development plan, and he could make no guarantees about results in one year's time.

Six months later, Dr. Clemens, reporting on progress, noted expenditures of $70,000 for salaries and equipment, only a start on the product development work, and only a moderate success with the oil color process. He reported that a major portion of the six months and the funds was spent in recruiting help, procuring equipments and supplies, and setting up the laboratory. Any real progress could not be expected during this initial period, but the company could expect something tangible at the end of the next six months.

Gus Nilsen had something new on his mind. He had been approached by a young mechanical engineer who had an idea for an ink marking pencil. The writing tip was actually the end of a wick which was saturated with colored ink. It would be more expensive than a crayon but had the advantage of better control over the thickness of the line drawn. A greater variety of colors could be made available, and the markings could be made more permanent by the use of indelible ink. Nilsen's questioned Clemens about developing such markers in his laboratory. If Dr. Clemens could do so, how much would it cost? If the costs were high, which way should the company go, with both development projects or one alone? If only one—which one?

Dr. Clemens did not have all the answers. He did know that neither he nor his technicians had the knowledge or ability to develop the indelible ink marker's mechanical features, and it would be necessary to hire a mechanical engineer, John McIntyre, to head this project, if the company decided to proceed with it. This would certainly increase the costs of research, since additional laboratory equipments would be needed. Dr. Clemens was inclined to think that the company could not afford to take on the new program. Production-minded Gus Nilsen felt that the progress obtained at a cost of $70,000 and six months time was an indication of failure, and that, probably, the oil color crayons project should be dropped and the indelible markers should be attempted instead.

To counter Nilsen's argument, Dr. Clemens suggested projections of calculations of return-on-investment for each project so that a decision could be made on a cost-effective basis. This computation was necessary anyway to establish standards for the control of the projects. The following data was collected for the calculations:

Oil Color Crayons

Laboratory equipment and fixtures	$50,000
Laboratory supplies/year	2,000
Research and development personnel/year	25,200
Wage increases and fringe benefits/year	7,000
Personnel costs (recruiting and administ.)	2,000
Operating cash required/year	20,000
Interest lost/year	800
Replacement and maintenance of lab. eqpt.	3,500
Estimated time for development	1.5 years
Additional production setup costs	$2,000
Estimated sales, 1st year	$50,000
2nd year	500,000
3rd year	$1,000,000

Indelible Markers

Additional laboratory equipment	$20,000
Laboratory supplies/year	3,000
Research and development personnel/year	15,600

Wage increases and fringe benefits/year	6,500
Personnel costs/year	2,000
Operating cash/year	15,000
Interest lost/year	600
Replacement and maintenance of lab. eqpt.	$4,000
Estimated time for development	2 years
Additional production setup costs	$100,000
Estimated sales, 1st year	75,000
2nd year	750,000
3rd year	$2,000,000

Both Projects

Laboratory equipment	$70,000
Laboratory supplies/year	5,000
R&D personnel/year	40,800
Wage increases and fringe benefits	13,500
Personnel administration/year	2,500
Operating cash/year	30,000
Interest lost/year	1,200
Lab. eqpt. replacem. and maintain.	$7,500
Completion of development	
Markers	2 years
Crayons	1 year
Added production setup costs	
1 year	$2,000
2 years	$100,000

Estimated Sales of New Products

1 year	$ 0
2 years	50,000
3 years	575,000
4 years	1,750,000
5 years	$3,000,000

Earnings (% of Sales) Prediction

Initial	5.0%
1st year	5.5
2nd year	5.5
3rd year	6.5
4th year	6.5
5th year	7.0

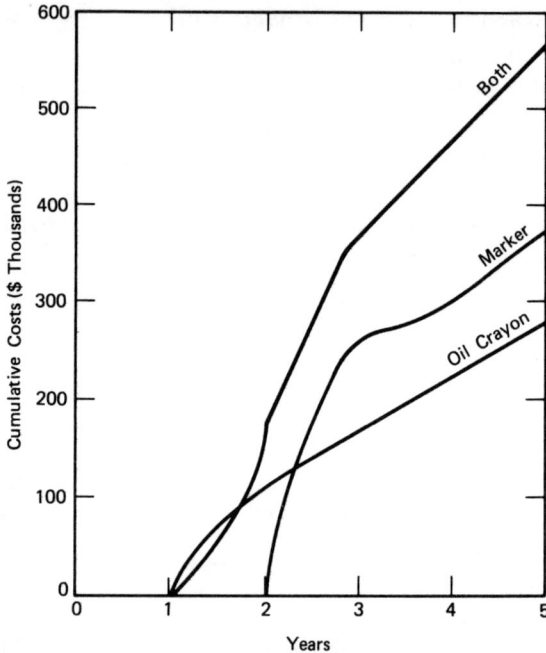

Figure 25 Cumulative Costs

The figures for both products developed are not always the sum of the individual costs. For example, the laboratory equipment already purchased for the oil crayons represent a fixed investment that exists even if it is desired to drop the oil crayon project. Personnel administration (recruiting) costs include large fixed costs that are not dependent on the number of personnel involved. Similarly, the cash needed for two projects is not much different from that required for one.

Curves can be plotted for the cumulative costs for the three alternatives; oil crayons, indelible markers, and both products (Figure 25).

There are no strong arguments for any of the alternatives. Dropping the oil crayon project will result in only a small saving in the total costs (from the inception). Carrying both projects means only 50% more costs not 100%. Each product costs approximately the same. If the oil crayon project had not been initiated earlier, the indelible marker would have been considerably less expensive. On the other hand, a substantial investment had already been made in the crayon project. This would be lost if it were dropped.

Curves are plotted for return-on-investment from the data in Table 5.10.

TABLE 5.10 THE GREASE PENCILS CORPORATION FINANCIAL DATA

	Cash	Cumulative Investment	Total Investment	Estimated Sales	Turnover	Earnings Rate	R.O.I. Rate
Oil Crayon							
1st yr.	—	—	—	—	—	—	0
2nd	$20,000	$111,500	$131,500	$ 50,000	0.38	0.06	0.023
3rd	20,000	170,000	190,000	500,000	2.63	0.065	0.17
4th	20,000	228,500	248,500	1,000,000	4.0	0.065	0.26
5th	20,000	287,000	307,000	1,000,000	3.25	0.07	0.23
Indelible Marker							
1st	—	—	—	—	—	—	0
2nd	—	—	—	—	—	—	0
3rd	15,000	261,900	276,900	75,000	0.27	0.065	0.018
4th	15,000	307,100	322,100	750,000	2.32	0.065	0.15
5th	15,000	382,300	367,300	2,000,000	5.44	0.07	0.38
Both Projects							
1st	—	—	—	—	—	—	0
2nd	30,000	177,900	207,900	50,000	0.24	0.06	0.014
3rd	30,000	373,900	403,900	575,000	1.42	0.065	0.09
4th	30,000	471,900	501,900	1,750,000	3.48	0.065	0.22
5th	$30,000	$569,900	$599,900	$3,000,000	5.0	0.07	0.35

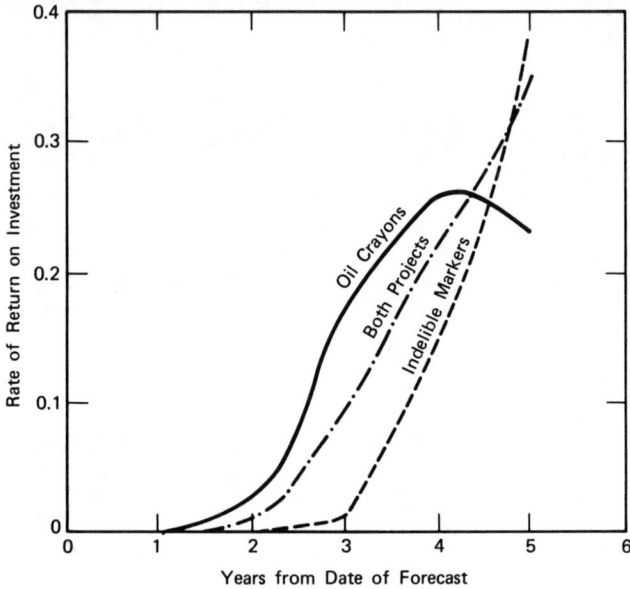

Figure 26   Return on Investment

It is apparent from the curves that the indelible markers will not do better than the oil crayons until 4.5 years after the date the estimates were made. It is, therefore, not advisable to replace the oil crayons project with the indelible markers project. The rate of return drops off after the fourth year for the oil crayons. It is evident that the crayons are an excellent short term investment, but the markers are better as a long term investment. The best policy is retaining both projects. Figure 26 can be used as control standards for the development and production of the two products.

CHAPTER 6

SHORT-INTERVAL SCHEDULING (SIS) AND DCR

Short-interval scheduling (SIS) is not a new idea. It has been in existence for more than 25 years, but it has received little publicity. While its main purpose is improving productivity, it is an excellent cost-reduction tool, capable of producing large savings in labor costs.

SHORT INTERVAL SCHEDULING (SIS) (1)

Essentially SIS replaces long term goals with short term goals. Thus, the company is free to use whatever work standards are best—historical, engineered, or none at all. SIS schedules are not completion standards but do need engineered work standards for maximum effectiveness.

SIS uses the relation between units of work and elements of time in a manner that alerts a supervisor to schedule variances at the earliest practical point while the work is being processed. Ordinarily, supervisors do not have exact knowledge of the number of types of operations at each work station, the work process time at each station, or the time when the work will be delivered by the process. SIS supplies this information and informs the supervisor about hourly conformance to schedule. He can then take action at the end of each hour. Otherwise the supervisor would not be aware of a problem until the normal reporting time, usually a week. By that time, a minor problem may have become a disaster.

The Unit of Work

The unit of work to be used as the measure of an activity is important. The unit needs to be a common denominator that does not vary. In production operations, the standard quantity of pieces per hour is a satisfactory unit.

For nonrepetitive activities such as maintenance, it is possible to establish an activity or a combination of activities that can be performed within the desired element of time. A small Los Angeles firm engaged in building maintenance (chiefly cleaning of offices) has been able to underbid the giants in its industry by carefully defining its work units and applying SIS.

In clerical activities, the unit of work may be a form, a ledger entry, and the like. For this form of activity, one must be careful that the activity measure is a true one. For example, date stamping a received order will always take the same amount of time. Processing the orders will take different times, depending on the number and type of items in the order. Classifying the orders by number and type of items would permit the establishment of a unit of work useful in SIS.

The work-time relationship does not need to be precise. The term used in SIS is *reasonable expectancy* (r/e). This is defined as the amount of work that an average employee can produce under normal work conditions in an hour. For example, suppose that incoming orders are routed to mail clerks, who date-stamp each order. After many measurements it is determined that 20 orders take an average of 4 minutes to stamp. Thus, it is established that a reasonable expectancy is 300 orders per hour. This can be verified by making a one hour measurement. The one hour result should be within 10 percent of the r/e. The r/e allows for the slack due to delays over which the worker has no control.

Selecting the Interval

The short interval need not be an hour, although an hour is the most common interval. The short interval can be longer or shorter, depending on the time it takes to complete an operation on a product or work item. Too short an interval requires too much of the supervisor's time to control the activity, but the time interval must be short enough so that corrective action can be taken before a variance affects the desired end result.

The interval must establish a realistic goal for the worker. The real secret of success of SIS is the establishment of short range objectives, because they increase the sense of urgency. With a long range objective, as a rule, the worker completes the greatest part of his task in the final days of his schedule, and quality is likely to be sacrificed. Break up the task into equal small increments, and he will be more likely to complete each increment on schedule. Remember, each of these smaller increments must be realistic goals, set by the man's normal pace or by engineered standards.

It is not sufficient to use SIS to control one small part of the total process. Date stamping an order does not complete its processing. It is necessary to synchronize all other activities connected with a received purchase order. It does no good to accelerate the mail room output to expedite the filling of orders if the order checkers' output is less than the desired number of orders per day. Manpower should be reshuffled so that areas with excessive output lose workers who are then shifted to areas with inadequate outputs.

Benefits of SIS

In the process of assigning manpower on an SIS controlled basis, it will become evident that much of the work can be accomplished by fewer people. This is the goal of SIS, the reduction of labor costs. One may decry the fact that SIS means a reduction in the labor force, but, without SIS, periodic layoffs are inevitable, sometimes on a large scale. Installing SIS will result in more employment stability for the workers. Maintaining a reasonably constant manpower level also reduces the rate paid for unemployment insurance.

Another important benefit of SIS is flexibility of job training received by workers. A conventional method is to write a very narrow job description and force a reasonably well-rounded individual into its confines. The company thus loses 40–60% of the overall potential of the people working there. Usually a work station is manned with people who do the same job day in and day out, even though volume changes drastically. These workers have not been trained in any other function, and there are no other workers trained to join them as needed. Monotony does not help morale.

What is needed is the application of the new people-oriented techniques of management—goal orientation, job enlargement, information feedback, flexible training and SIS. These will make it possible to present an assignment to a work crew, allow them to decide how to complete it, and measure their progress. The crew will keep their supervisor informed and let him know how he can help. This working environment can bring about as much as 25% gains in productivity, with profit gains of much larger magnitudes.

Selling SIS

A major obstacle to the success of SIS in most organizations is resistance to anything new or different, particularly when it affects jobs. The problem is that SIS is not understood at the lower management levels.

SIS must be sold. All involved must be shown that the program will benefit the employees, their supervision, and the company. The hardest to convince are often the supervisors. They must be involved in the SIS planning, establishment of units of measure, reasonable estimates, and the like. Supervisors must understand that SIS has nothing to do with individual worker productivity but is merely a tool for the management of time.

It goes without saying that union officials should be briefed in advance of SIS installations. With unions, it should be stressed that SIS uses either established work standards, or the pace workers themselves set. Any layoffs that may be required will enhance the security of the workers that remain. The layoffs would be temporary, because lower costs will permit the company to grow, creating new jobs.

Example: The Cheseborough Company order processing department is organized as follows:

Order editing	4 editors
Tax application	1 clerk
Routing section	2 clerks
Order typing	2 typists
Order checking	2 checkers
Total	11 people

The first step in an SIS program is to establish the unit of work and the unit of time for work measurement. In this example, the obvious choice for the unit of work is an order. Unfortunately, the orders are of different size and complexity. Customers differ in the manner in which they order; sometimes orders are neatly typed on order blanks and others may be scribbled on scraps of paper. The orders can be sorted into types, according to the time it takes to process them. This categorizing can be done in two ways: actual work measurement (i.e., time study) or averaging of historical data. The latter is accomplished by observing the operation over a long period of time. This is not recommended, because the work standard is established by the worker. What is needed is the pace at which the job *can be done*.

TABLE 6.1 CHESEBOROUGH WORK SCHEDULE

Daily Volume Report
Order Processing Department

Activity	Prev. Day Balance	Orders Recvd.	Date: _June 20_ Completed	Incompleted
Editing	20	200	190	30
Tax Applic.	0	190	125	65
Routing	50	240	240	50
Typing	30	240	150	120
Checking	0	150	150	0
Totals	100	1020	855	265

When time study is impractical or not desirable, the average of observations over a long period will have to do. The average should be in units per hour and is the reasonable expectancy of performance. When engineered standards are available, the reasonable expectancy will be the standard hour, plus an allowance for unexpected and unavoidable delays.

Table 6.1 is the conventionable type of work scheduling that was used at Cheseborough for the ordering department. The total orders received is actually the number of orders multiplied by the number of activities.

Note that this table gives no clue about why the department failed to process all the orders received. There is no way to determine whether the department is adequately staffed, because there is no information about the nature of the orders or whether the workers' performance is normal or abnormal.

Table 6.2 is a suggested form for a table used in testing to

TABLE 6.2 CHESEBOROUGH WORK MEASUREMENT CHART

Order Processing Department Editing Activity

Order Type	First Period Start	End	Number Compl.	Units Per Hour	Second Period Start	End	Number Compl.	Units Per Hour
A	8:00	8:30	12	24	9:10	9:20	3	18
B	8:30	8:40	5	31	9:20	9:40	10	33
C	8:40	8:50	10	62	9:40	10:00	19	60
D	8:50	9:10	2	6	10:00	10:30	4	8

establish performance standards. In this case no engineered standards are available.

One hour has been selected as a realistic time unit for the SIS program, since each operation on orders is completed in a matter of minutes. Two test periods do not really yield enough data for a reliable and reasonable expectancy but are sufficient to demonstrate the method. The reasonable expectancy for each of the order types is computed as follows:

A orders: units per hour per number of periods $= (24 + 18)/2$
$$= 42/2 = 21$$

Because there are four editors: $21/4 = 5.25$
orders per hour per editor

B orders: $(31 + 33)/2 = 64/2 = 32$
$32/4 = 8$ orders per hour per editor
C orders: $(62 + 60)/2 = 122/2 = 61$
$61/4 = 15.25$ orders per hour per editor
D orders: $(6 + 8)/2 = 14/2 = 7$
$7/4 = 1.75$ orders per hour per editor

TABLE 6.3 SIS SCHEDULES FOR ORDER EDITING ACTIVITY

Chart 1. Forecast of Volume and Hours

Date: June 20 Type	R/E	Orders Recd.	Reqd. Proc. Hours	Actual Hours
A	21	96	4.57	
B	32	180	5.63	
C	61	360	5.9	
D	7	42	6.0	
Total		678	22.1	23.4

Available hours, 4 editors, 8 hours each = 32.0
Excess = 32.0 − 23.4 = 8.6 hours

Chart 2. SIS Schedule

Type	R/E	Editor	Orders Assign.	Scheduled Start	Finish	Actual Hours	Diff. Hours
A	5.25	Smith	32	8:00 AM	2:30 PM	3:30 PM	$+1$
A	5.25	Jones	32	8:00 AM	2:30 PM	2:00 PM	$-\frac{1}{2}$
A	5.25	Harris	32	8:00 AM	2:30 PM	1:00 PM	$+\frac{1}{2}$

The next step is to prepare an SIS schedule for the order editing activity. The capacity of individual workers will vary considerably from day to day. Therefore we need to concern ourselves with the group and not with the output of individuals. Several possible charts are available as SIS schedules. The choice of schedule will depend on the needs and wishes of the supervisor of the activity. Table 6.3 demonstrates two forms of the SIS schedule.

Chart 1 is suitable for the start of the SIS program. It serves as a verification of the unit of measurement testing and, in addition, establishes how many workers are needed for a particular activity. The estimate forecast shows that 22.1 hours are needed to process a total of 678 orders. Actual time required is 23.4 hours. This confirms that the expectancy figure is reasonable and that only three editors are needed instead of four. We begin to see the value of SIS even before we attempt to control the activity, because we can schedule work assignments with precision. We know exactly how many orders each man can process.

Chart 2 is the kind we would use to control the activity, the implementation of the SIS program. Based on Chart 1, we have assigned three men to the editing tasks, and we use the single editor expectancy rate. The scheduled start and finish time is determined by the required hours for processing from the expectancy rate. We find that Jones and Harris complete their work within 10 percent of the scheduled time. However, Smith takes about 17 percent more time. The supervisor must determine the cause and make the suitable correction or adjustment.

An additional benefit that accrues from Chart 1 is the determination of the true capacity of each station. This permits the elimination of bottlenecks. For example, knowing that the capacities are as follows:

Order editing	4 editors	700 orders per day
Tax application	1 clerk	500 orders per day
Routing section	2 clerks	600 orders per day
Typing	2 typists	300 orders per day
Checking	2 checkers	400 orders per day

and that the number of orders received on a specific day are 500, reassignments can be made to ensure the processing of all the orders without overloading or underloading excessively any of the stations. The new assignments for the day would be as follows:

		Capacity
Order editing	3 editors	525
Tax application	1 clerk	500
Routing	1 full, 1 half time	450
Typing	3 typists	450
Checking	2 full, 1 half time	600
Total	11 people	

Assuming all the people are trained in all operations, the fourth editor would spend one half of his time in the routing section and the other half in order checking. Where previously the department would have been limited to 300 orders for the day, the capacity of the order typists, now the department can handle 450 orders. Further, people from order editing and order checking, with excess capacity, can help the routing section and order typing to get the other 50 orders through the 450 order capacity stations.

Both Charts 1 and 2 represent only a small sampling of the variations in SIS schedule charts that are possible. However, all such charts contain the same basic data arranged differently.

There are some very important considerations that cannot be overlooked when attempting to apply SIS to clerical or office workers. The chief item is wasted time, both overt and covert. To some extent, wasted time can be found in all repetitive tasks, particularly on the production line.

Overt lost time is that time during which employees are not performing any productive work. Management is at fault when the lost time is due to poor scheduling, tool and machinery failures, and over-hiring (manpower for peak loads instead of average load). Clerical operations are more likely to suffer from excessive "breaks". It is possible to find, even in a well managed office, employees in idle conversation, visiting friends in other areas, wandering off from their work stations, and taking unscheduled coffee breaks. Such lost time rarely occurs when a supervisor is present. It is necessary to determine the amount of overt lost time in order to obtain reliable reasonable estimates of productivity for implementing SIS. There are various means of detecting this type of lost time.

1. The observer (usually the supervisor) stations himself where most of the people can be observed. The observer will be occupied with some task. The unscheduled breaks will not occur until the workers

become accustomed to the presence of the observer (usually about an hour). When conditions have settled down to "normal", the observer can begin. The first step is to obtain a head count of the total number of workers under observation. Next, the observer will determine the percentage of lost time at any time by counting the number not working and dividing that number by the total number of workers in the area. This is done for about 20 intervals during a two hour period, and an average is taken of all the percentages. The result will be an estimate of the lost time.

2. Another method is to observe the group for several hours and count the man-minutes lost. Dividing the total man-minutes into the total minutes of idle time will give the lost time percentage.

3. The observer can count the number of people not working as he walks through the area. An average can be taken of counts made at various times during the day over a period of several days.

The next question is how to reduce the overt lost time or, more properly, whether it should be reduced. Unscheduled coffee breaks are the office worker's status symbol. They distinguish him from blue collar workers and place him in the same class as professionals and managers. Any attempt to curtail such practices will seriously affect the morale of the office. Note that office employees are only temporarily embarassed in the presence of a supervisor, but very soon return to their normal routine.

Though it would be bad practice to curtail the breaks, it is good practice to control them. Control must be firm, but not obtrusive. SIS with short term, achievable goals is that type of control. In addition to control, there must be morale boosters to replace the need for the breaks. This would take the form of making the work less monotonous (through flexibility of assignments) and more challenging (requiring more skill, identifying with important products or programs, stressing importance of the work, etc). Since this type of lost time may run as high as 30% of the clerical payroll, it is worthwhile to find some ways to reduce the 30% to a more reasonable figure of 10%.

Covert Lost Time

This kind of lost time is difficult to detect and measure. It takes three forms.

1. *Procedures.* As a company grows, so do its rules, regulations, policies, and procedures, each of which sprouts a bewildering array of forms and controls. Add to this a complex network of interoffice

communications and an expensive and busy copymaking machine. Experts who specialize in procedures engineering will, for a fee, make the system more "efficient." They concern themselves with the shortest paths for the routing of documents, minimizing the mail clerk's mileage, and rearranging the format of the forms. In the process, some cost reductions will accrue, because of this concentration on how things are done. But a far greater reduction in clerical costs can be achieved by eliminating all unnecessary paperwork. We must question why something is being done and the question must not be asked of the clerks who do that "something." An objective answer is needed from someone who is familiar with company operations as a whole.

2. *Parkinson's Law.* Invariably, clerical employees make the work at hand fill up the available time. This inefficiency is usually caused by the failure of management to provide sufficient work for the employees. More precisely, it follows from the practice of hiring specialists without carefully analyzing the true needs of the operation. For example, a filing clerk is hired to relieve an overworked typist of a tedious, time consuming chore, although a study of the work load may show that filing takes no more than 10% of the typist's time. One cannot blame the file clerk for stretching out the work to avoid idleness and the possible loss of a job.

3. *Large Work Variances.* Workers are human and therefore unlikely to maintain a uniform pace. However, the range of variance in the individual pace is usually not large. Whenever the variance is exceptionally wide, there is a possibility of lost time. We are not concerned with the difference in pace between individuals. There is no average person. When we talk of average productivity, we are averaging atypical outputs. It is conceivable that an office may be staffed by a preponderance of lazy people, and the average productivity may be considerably lower than that from a comparable office down the hall. Our concern is with the variances in each individual employee's pace. To detect this covert waste requires a different approach.

One method of finding the lost time is to observe a person at work for 20 to 30 minutes without the employee's knowledge on four or five separate occasions. Record the output for each of these occasions. Now do one measurement during which the employee is aware of your presence. The employee is certain to produce at his normal rate while under observation. Use the normal rate obtained to evaluate his productivity when he is not aware of an observer. Large variances may be an indication of lost time.

An easier way to detect variances is to count the batches of work accomplished in a day, convert to pieces per hour, and compare this figure with the rate obtained when the clerk knew he was being observed. Variances as high as 10% are not significant. It is the variances of 50–60% that are being sought. Variances many times larger than that are not unusual.

Causes of Covert Lost Time

It is convenient to talk about the average worker, and a great deal of research has gone into defining who this means. The inevitable conclusion is that the average worker is a myth. His description varies with the researcher. Time-and-motion studies have tried to treat man as a machine, often with disastrous results, because the workers band together to protect the slowest among them and to keep the price of their labor high. The fact is that there are wide differences between the productivity of workers for the same operation. The reasons for the differences may be physical, psychological or both.

The advantage of SIS is that it does not attempt to impose any outsider's standards but uses the average productivity of the group under analysis. The reasonable estimate of productivity takes into account the individual variances. The estimate may be low, because of a preponderance of new and unskilled employees, or high, because the members of the group are all senior, experienced workers. It is quite possible, therefore, that a change in the makeup of the group may account for an apparent increase in lost time. As a result the reasonable estimate should be verified at regular intervals. When trying to measure the lost time one should learn as much as possible about the people involved. Past performances should be considered.

For new employees, it would be helpful to know approximately when they should be up to par. By par, we do not mean some mythical average productivity. We are not interested in how much the worker can produce, but in the length of time it will take a worker to reach *his or her* peak output. In other words, the worker will be measured against his own standard. Then, when measuring the output of a group, we can rate the group on the basis of where each member stands in relation to his or her learning curve. Then and only then is it possible to realistically detect covert lost time.

To minimize the measurement effort, instead of plotting a learning curve for every worker, one should plot curves for, say, ten workers, then average these curves. The average is the reasonable estimate for that operation.

Two important causes of lost time are a backlog of work or the lack of a backlog. It is an odd fact that both these conditions have the same demoralizing effect on a work force. A worker or a group of workers will soon decide that it is a waste of time to try to catch up when faced with a backlog that never seems to change. On the other hand, constantly running out of work will have similar deleterious effects. If workers are not worried about their jobs, they will stretch out the work. The solution for both cases is to use SIS to control backlogs.

SIS Applied To Maintenance

Maintenance is usually considered a nonrepetitive activity, and it is rarely scheduled or controlled. The truth is that most maintenance tasks are repetitive. Machine failures can be predicted. There is a limited number of failure modes for all engineered products. The isolation of the fault is a well-defined technique and can be readily timed for scheduling. The correction of the problem is also readily timed.

The military, in purchasing equipment, long ago established a science of "maintainability" stemming from their concern over maintenance costs. The military's problem is multiplied by the complexity of the machines they purchase and their severe reliability requirements. What we can learn from them is how to measure and control maintenance work. Military specifications contain a specified equipment downtime for maintenance (also referred to as "time to return to service" or "repair time"). The specifications recognize that the length of the downtime varies considerably from one failure to another. By analysis of experimental data, it has been established that the range of downtime is such that downtime can be estimated by probability theory.

Figure 27 demonstrates how closely the theoretical approaches the actual downtime. The "actual" data were gathered from maintenance work by two different crews operating on 24 systems. The purpose of showing the curves here is to prove that work measures are feasible for maintenance. The data collected for the curves have their parallel in the SIS reasonable estimate of productivity.

The lesson to be learned from the maintainability discipline is the treatment of all maintenance costs and the methodology for minimizing these costs.

Cost of Setting Up Periodic Maintenance

The major factor contributing to this cost is the downtime of the system that results from the preparations required for performing the periodic

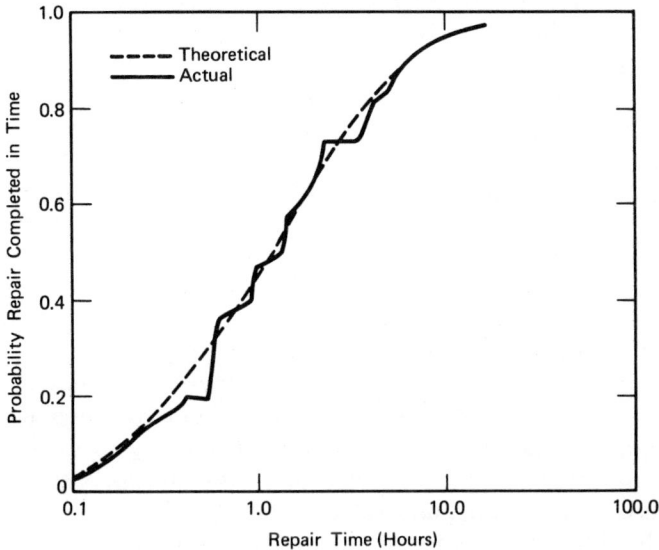

Figure 27   Probability of Repair

maintenance. Other costs are those for labor and materials specifically required for setups, but these are usually negligible compared to the cost of downtime. The setup cost is incurred each time periodic maintenance is performed, and it is relatively independent of the actual items inspected.

A crew of maintenance men is usually kept for the specific purpose of maintaining the plant equipment in an operating or ready condition. They perform such tasks as scheduled inspection, preventive repair of deteriorated items, emergency diagnosis and repair of failed items, and routine tasks necessary to keep test equipment, tools, and spares in serviceable condition. The costs incurred in support of these men are relatively fixed. They are required to provide a capability of performing the maintenance function, and the cost depends primarily on the number of men and their skills. SIS can be used effectively in the reduction of this cost.

For our purpose, we will view maintenance as a variable cost. This differs from the concept of maintenance as a fixed cost, with preventive maintenance to be performed whenever no other work is available. We will consider *total* maintenance costs, which include all costs—preventive maintenance, downtime, emergency repairs, and the like.

It is difficult to establish the frequency of periodic inspections for preventive maintenance on a system composed of many types of machines, because each type has its own failure rate. Because of the downtime and setup cost for each inspection, it is advisable to schedule more than one machine each time the system is down. This minimizes the downtime costs.

The manpower available for a periodic inspection determines the rate at which items can be inspected and repaired. The downtime for preventive maintenance can be decreased by increasing the manpower applied to the tasks. The optimum level of manpower depends on the relative cost of manpower and downtime.

The cost of the manpower can be reduced by applying SIS. The cost of the downtime can be reduced by scheduling preventive maintenance for hours when the plant is normally closed. Such scheduling will usually increase the cost of maintenance manpower. However, if SIS has minimized manpower costs, the overtime costs are negligible compared to the savings in downtime costs.

By scheduling the inspection of items before the expected time of failure, the number of failures and the associated costs of unscheduled system downtime, emergency repair, and the like, can be reduced sufficiently to offset the costs of scheduled maintenance. The problem is to select the time between periodic inspections and to select the items to receive preventive inspection at each succeeding periodic inspection in such a way that maintenance costs are minimized. The solutions to this problem and the corresponding minimum cost depend on the available manpower and its efficient use. Therefore, it is necessary to find the manpower level that gives the least maintenance costs for the level of system operation required and to ensure efficient use of the manpower through SIS.

For each preventive inspection of an item, there is an inspection cost. If a repair is made during an inspection, then there is a cost of preventive repair. If the item fails before its next scheduled inspection, the cost of the failure includes both a repair cost and a downtime cost. The cost of a failure usually exceeds the costs associated with preventive maintenance for the item. This is the reason that preventive maintenance is so important for keeping maintenance costs low.

If preventive maintenance does not involve any repairs, the cost of the preventive maintenance is the inspection costs alone. This is often called the *marginal cost* of preventive maintenance.

The condition of the item at the time of an inspection and the length of time between inspections determines the probability of a repair being needed.

Example: The decision to repair is made at the time of the inspection. An item that fails between preventive inspections is repaired immediately. At the inspection, there are three possibilities.

Condition	Action
Good	None
Deteriorated	Repair at next inspection
Failed	Repair immediately

The probability of any one of these conditions varies as the number of periodic inspections.

The annual maintenance and repair costs for an item are given by

$$C_i = (C_1/T + C_2 P/T + C_3 E/T) \times 52 \text{ weeks}$$

where C_i = annual maintenance costs for an item
C_1 = marginal cost of preventive inspection
C_2 = cost of preventive repair
C_3 = failure cost
T = time between inspections in weeks
P = probability of a preventive repair
E = probability of a failure

The total maintenance costs are given by

$$C_t = \text{total} = 52C_0/T + C_M + \text{sum of all } C_i\text{s}$$

where C_t = total annual maintenance costs
C_0 = preventive setup costs
C_M = manpower costs/year (maintenance only)

Manpower costs are also present in each C_i in the following manner:

$$C_1 = (W_1/M)C_D$$

$$C_2 = (W_2/M)C_D$$

where W_1 = average manhours for preventive inspection of the item
W_2 = average manhours for preventive repair of the item

M = number of maintenance men
C_D = cost of system downtime

The cost of a failure is given by

$$C_3 = C_D D$$

where D = average time for emergency diagnosis and repair of the item

Given the following data:

W_1 = 4 manhours
W_2 = 6 manhours
M = 2
C_M = \$5000 per year per man
C_D = \$500 per hour
D = 10 hours
T = 2 weeks
P = 0.9
E = 0.1
C_O = \$50 per inspection

Find C_t for this item.

$C_1 = (W_1/M)C_D = 4/2 \times \$500 = \$1000$
$C_2 = 6/2 \times \$500 = \$1500$
$C_3 = 10 \times \$500 = \$5000$
$C_i = 52[\$1000/2 + (\$1500 \times 0.9)/2 + (\$5000 \times 0.1)/2]$
$\quad = 52 \times \$1425 = \$74,100$
$C_t = 52 \times 50/2 + \$5000 + \$74,100 = \$1300 + \$5000 = \$74,100$
$\quad = \$80,400$

Janitorial Services

Firms that provide contractual janitorial services have for a long time been applying SIS in order to be able to compete not only with other such firms, but also with inhouse janitorial crews. They probably do not call it SIS, but it is very definitely a very fine form of the technique. Most companies still using full time employees for cleaning offices and factories make no attempt to control the work of such employees, nor is there any attempt to analyze the cost of such service. There should be. Even a cursory examination will find:

1. Excessive payroll costs. One should ask for a proposal from a janitorial contractor and compare his payroll for that service.
2. Excessive supplies cost. Inefficient methods, plus uncontrolled supplies procurement, result in tremendous waste.

TABLE 6.4 TYPICAL JANITORIAL SCHEDULE

Start Time_____	Stop Time_____		Supvr. Check_____		
Procedure	Est. Time Reqd. (min)	No. Of Items	Total Est. Time (min)	Actual Time	Notes
Empty waste baskets	2	25	50		
Empty and clean ashtrays	2	20	40		
Sweep floors	5	25	125		
Sweep hall	10	1	10		
Dust desks	1	25	25		
Total			250 = 4 hours, 10 minutes		

3. Large investment in cleaning equipment. Aside from the expenditure of a sizable amount of capital, a company is tied to equipment that is rapidly made obsolete by new and more efficient machines.

The contractors, from long experience, have established reasonable estimates of how long it takes to perform any cleaning task. These estimates are as detailed as "2 minutes to clean an ashtray". They devise procedures for each man so that there will be no waste motion. Also, they establish schedules not only for the daily cleaning requirements, but also for the entire year. For example, some tasks are completed daily, others at various longer intervals (like waxing floors, cleaning blackboards, etc.). A typical janitorial schedule is shown in Table 6.4.

All of this is particularly applicable to the maintenance of hotels, motels, large apartment complexes, and similar facilities.

SIS Applied To Research

Productivity can not be measured in the area of research, except for support services. However, the principles of SIS can be applied to research planning. Ordinarily, the time and dollar schedules prepared for study proposals and for research project planning are estimates of the *total* time to complete the work. In essence, a long range goal is provided for the engineers. It has been demonstrated that long range goals do not provide sufficient motivation to anyone, whether scientist or laborer, to expedite the task at hand. Replace the long range goal with a short term one and the goal is moved into reach. The effect of misuse of time is felt immediately, and it is therefore more painful.

The worker with long range goals is insulated from the impact of wasted time by many layers of time between him and the end of the project.

Estimates submitted by supervisors for engineering groups are usually in hundreds of manhours or even manmonths. The supervisor could not have arrived at the estimate without having first obtained estimates on subtask hours from his engineers or from his own experience. These subtasks, in turn, are based on further estimates on increments of the subtask. Thus we see that the elements of SIS do exist in the research department, but they are not set down in black and white. It is management's fault if it does not make full use of the existing, unwritten SIS.

The first step is to refuse lump sum estimates of manpower requirements and then to demand a breakdown in terms of project accomplishments. The immediate advantage is that the estimates are more readily challenged, resulting in more realistic estimates. For example, no one can argue with an estimate of six manmonths to study the feasibility of a new radar receiver design. On the other hand, 40 manhours to flight-test the receiver will appear to be too low, unless there is some explanation for the low estimate.

Whether preparing an initial estimate or a project plan, the procedure for short interval control is as follows:

1. Break the overall task into subtasks.
2. Determine all the work to be done to complete each subtask.
3. Establish the time requirements for each incremental job of the subtasks.
4. Break these requirements down into schedules for people.
5. Establish the interim goals and incremental goals.
6. Create a short range schedule for each goal, based on SIS principles by matching schedule to available manpower, defining pace setting tasks, avoiding bottlenecks, and the like.
7. Break the schedule into logical check points.
8. Check the accomplishment against the plan at each checkpoint.
9. Take corrective action to get back on the track, if the actual accomplishment falls short of the plan.

SIS AND PERT

PERT, PERT/COST, and CPM are time-network analysis techniques developed for planning and controlling large programs. They can be

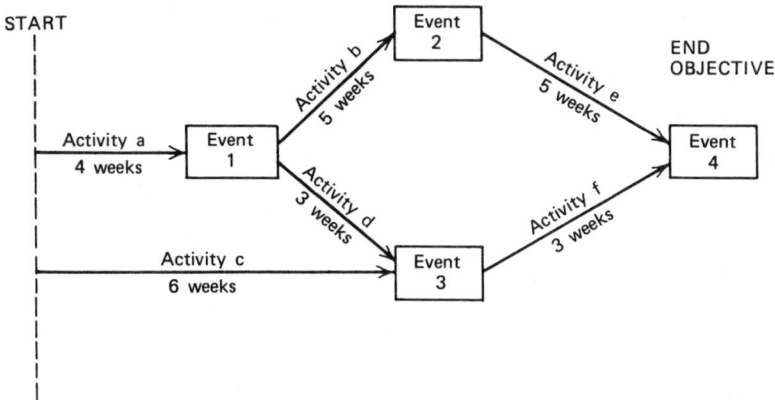

Figure 28   PERT Network

considered an overall control device for every facet of the operation, from sales to delivery of the product. SIS is used for controlling individual components of the whole. The control of the whole depends on the ability to control each component part.

Program Evaluation Review Technique (PERT) presents tasks, events, and activities in a network in sequential form with time estimates. A typical PERT network is shown in Figure 28.

Each arrow or activity in this network represents one of the various planned tasks or jobs leading to the End Objective and requires expenditures of resources, such as time, labor, and material. The boxes at the beginning and end of the activity arrows are events or milestones in the PERT network. An event is a definable point in time, and it signifies a decision to start or terminate an activity or job. An event, unlike an activity, does not require the expenditure of resources. An event is used, for example, to identify the point in time at which funds are released, a contract awarded, or an item delivered.

After the network activity and event relationships are developed, the time required to accomplish each activity is estimated and noted on the network. For example, in Figure 28, it has been estimated that activity *a* will require 4 weeks, activity *b* 5 weeks, and so forth. Each activity must be accompanied by a time estimate in order to make proper use of the network. We can see, for example, that activities *a* and *c* can be started simultaneously, but activity *f* cannot be started until activities *c* and *d* are completed.

Starting from "START", we now compute the earliest date by which each event can be expected to be completed. For example, activity *a* is expected to take 4 weeks. Therefore, Event 1 may be accomplished in

4 weeks. In the case of Event 3, tasks *a, c,* and *d* must be completed before Event 3 is accomplished. We must use the longest path for this estimate (measured from the beginning of *c*). The longest path is *a* plus *d,* or 7 weeks. Similarly, the time estimate for Event 4, the END OBJECTIVE, is the longest path *a* plus *b* plus *c,* or 14 weeks.

It is also important to know the latest allowable time by which each activity must be accomplished if Event 4 is not to occur more than 14 weeks after "START". This is computed by successively subtracting the activity time estimates in reverse sequence. For example, 14 weeks minus the 3 weeks of *f* gives 11 weeks, which means that Event 3 must be completed in 11 weeks from "START". But activity *c* takes 6 weeks, and *a* plus *d* takes 7 weeks—the longest path. Therefore, there is a 4 week cushion or slack for Event 3.

The latest allowable time for Event 2 is 9 weeks. Observe that the estimated time for Event 2 is exactly 9 weeks from "START". This means zero slack time. Thus, we have identified the *critical path* on the network (zero slack) as *a* plus *b* plus *e.* The activities and events on this path effectively establish and control the time to reach the END OBJECTIVE, Event 4. Slippage of any event on this path will equally delay the end objective.

The critical path is said to be *pacing*, because it is the minimum time for completion, and its modification will decide whether the scheduled date for completion will be met.

If SIS is not being used, the time estimates for PERT are pure guesses, even when provided by the activity's supervisor. To assess the risk taken in performing the job, a time estimate with a probability of .5 is computed as follows:

Three estimates are obtained:

a = time that the activity will take if everything to be done is done successfully the first time (optimistic estimate).

m = the time required to accomplish an activity under normal circumstances, with some success and some failure (most likely estimate).

b = the time the activity will take with extremely bad luck (pessimistic estimate).

The 50% probability expected time is found from the formula

$$(a + 4m + b)/6$$

The result is an average of the three estimates.

If we now apply SIS, we can eliminate *b,* the pessimistic estimate, because of the tighter control. We know that *a* is a very unlikely situation. That leaves m as the *reasonable estimate* obtained through SIS. It has a tolerance of about plus or minus 10%. We can call this a probability of .90, a considerable improvement over the time estimate without SIS.

Example: The polishing and plating of trim for a microwave oven is an activity for which the following time estimates have been made before SIS is installed:

> Optimistic, a = 3 weeks
> Most likely, m = 5 weeks
> Pessimistic, b = 12 weeks

The time estimate is computed from

$$(a + 4m + b)/6 = (3 + 20 + 12)/6 = 6 \text{ weeks}$$

The labor costs for this plating operation are $2000 per week. The cost estimate is cost per week multiplied by the estimated time for completion.

$$\$2000 \times 6 = \$12,000$$

This estimate is not high enough because the probability of completion is only .5. It probably will take considerably more time to complete the work—perhaps as much as 12 weeks, the pessimistic estimate. A reasonable guess is that the best estimate would fall about half-way between the computed estimate of 6 weeks and the pessimistic one of 12 weeks. This would make 9 weeks a safe estimate and the cost estimate, 9 × $2,000 or $18,000.

With SIS, the time estimate becomes the most likely estimate—5 weeks. The cost estimate is then 5 × $2,000 or $10,000. Since the tolerance on the SIS estimate is ±10%, this cost estimate should be increased to $11,000. This is a reduction of $7,000 (from $18,000) in the pricing of the ovens. Similar or greater savings can be realized in the rest of the operations in the manufacture of the ovens.

SUMMARY

Essentially, SIS replaces long term goals with short term goals. Normally, it is applied to increasing productivity but it is useful to control many types of costs in a DCR program.

SIS uses the relation between units of work and elements of time in a manner that alerts a supervisor to schedule variances at the earliest practical point, while the work is being processed. Ordinarily, supervisors do not have exact knowledge of the number of types of operations at each work station, work process time at each station, or the time when the work will be delivered by the process. SIS supplies this information and informs the supervisor about hourly conformance to schedule. He can then take action at the end of each hour. Otherwise he would not be aware of a problem until the normal reporting time, usually a week. By that time, a minor problem may have become a disaster.

The unit of work to be used as the measure of an activity is important. In production operations, the standard quantity of pieces per hour is a satisfactory unit. For nonrepetitive activities such as maintenance, it is possible to establish an activity or a combination of activities that can be performed within the desired element of time. In clerical activities, the unit of work may be a form, a ledger entry, and the like.

The work-time relationship in SIS is called the reasonable expectancy (r/e), which is defined as the amount of work that an average employee can produce under normal work conditions in an hour. The short time-interval commonly used is an hour. The interval must establish a realistic goal for the worker.

The secret of success for SIS is the establishment of short range objectives, because they increase the sense of urgency. With a long range objective the worker is likely to complete the greatest part of his task in the final days of his schedule, and quality is likely to be sacrificed.

There are some very important considerations that cannot be overlooked when attempting to apply SIS to clerical or office workers. The chief item is wasted time, both overt and covert. Overt lost time is that time during which employees are not performing any productive work. Covert lost time is due to items such as unnecessary paperwork, Parkinson's law, large work variances, and the like.

The average worker is a myth whose description varies with the researcher. The fact is that there are wide differences between the productivity of workers in the same operation because of physical and/or psychological differences.

Maintenance is usually considered a nonrepetitive activity and it is rarely scheduled or controlled. The truth is that most maintenance tasks are repetitive. Machine failures can be predicted (there is a limited number of failure modes for all engineered products). The isolation of the fault is a well-defined technique and can be readily timed for scheduling. The correction of the problem is also readily timed. The military includes maintenance schedules in the specifications for the equipment it buys.

A major factor in maintenance costs is the downtime of the system. Downtime can be estimated with accuracy.

The cost of maintenance manpower can be reduced by applying SIS. The cost of the downtime can be reduced by scheduling preventive maintenance for hours when the plant is normally closed.

The total annual maintenance costs are given by the sum

$$\frac{\text{Number preventive maintenance setups} \times \text{Cost of setup}}{\text{Time between inspections}}$$
+ Maintenance manpower costs per year
+ Annual total maintenance costs

The principles of SIS can be applied to research planning. Conventional time and dollar schedules for research or engineering are estimates of the total time to complete the work. In essence, a long range goal is provided for the engineers. Long range goals do not provide sufficient motivation to expedite the task at hand.

Estimates submitted by supervisors for engineering groups are usually in hundreds of manhours or even manmonths. Supervisor estimates are based on subtask estimates from his engineers or from his own experience. These subtasks, in turn, are based on further estimates on increments of the subtask. Lump sum estimates of manpower requirements should be refused and a breakdown in terms of project accomplishments requested.

PERT, PERT/COST, and CPM are time-network analysis techniques developed for planning and controlling large programs. They can be considered an overall control device for every facet of the operation, from sales to delivery of the product. SIS can be used to control individual components of the whole. The control of the whole depends on the ability to control each component part. The 50% probability expected time (for a PERT network) is found in the same formula used in Chapter 2 to obtain an average of three estimates (optimistic, pessimistic, and most likely). If SIS is used, the pessimistic estimate can be eliminated because of the tighter control. We know that the optimistic estimate is a very unlikely situation. That leaves the most likely estimate as the *reasonable estimate* obtained through SIS. It has a tolerance of about ±10%. We can call this a probability of .90, which is a considerable improvement over the time estimate without SIS.

REFERENCES

1. R. J. Behan, *"Cost Reduction Through Short Interval Scheduling,"* Prentice-Hall, Englewood Cliffs, New Jersey, 1966.

SIS CASE STUDIES

The heart of DCR is the setting of *feasible* goals and objectives. SIS is an extremely important tool for this purpose. It is for this reason that the variety of SIS case studies that follow are presented. The material on maintenance cost optimization is only indirectly related to SIS, but this does not make it any the less important to the success of a DCR program.

THE APEX COMPANY

Production planning in the Apex Company is accomplished by issuing a weekly schedule to each department. Table 6.5 is a sample of such a production schedule. The planner's control consists of receiving daily output reports and giving each foreman a daily report showing the actual output compared with the plan.

No corrections were ever made and the planner was forced to reschedule continuously.

There are many problems with this kind of schedule:

1. No time requirements.
2. No station loading.
3. Setup and run times not separated.
4. No priorities established.

TABLE 6.5   PRODUCTION SCHEDULE

| Week of: Jan. 13 | | Department: Plating |
Part Number	Tank Number	Quantity
1340	3	2000
1016	2	3000
1502	4	1000
1543	1	4000
1550	6	2000
1400	5	4000

TABLE 6.6 PRODUCTION SCHEDULE

			Hours	
Week of: Feb. 12			Department: Plating	
Available hours all tanks: 38				
Available plater hours: 190				
Part Number	Quantity	Pieces Per Hour	Setup	Run
Tank 1				
1200	4,000	500	4.0	8.0
1112	10,000	500	6.0	20.0
Tank 2				
1450	10,000	500	3.5	20.0
1400	5,000	500	7.0	10.0
Tank 3				
1310	2,000	75	4.0	30.0
Tank 4				
1550	2,000	75	6.0	30.0
Tank 5				
1560	1,400	40	3.5	35.0
Tank 6				
1600	3,600	100	3.5	36.0
Totals			37.0	189.0

5. No manpower requirements.
6. Requirements and capacity not matched.

Apex hired an industrial engineer to solve their production problems. He began by studying the plating operation. This department had one setup man and five operators. Using the work standards data he collected, he prepared the production schedule of Table 6.6.

The table lists the various rates at which each part can be plated, the quantities of each part to be plated, the time required for plating setup for each quantity of parts, the run times, and the total time required for both setup and plating. The industrial engineer hoped that this table would give him:

1. Required tank time.
2. Matching of available labor to tank time.
3. Separation of setup and run required times.
4. Comparison between scheduled hours and capacity.
5. Reasonable expectancy.

TABLE 6.7 SCHEDULE COMPUTATIONS

Part	Tank 1 Setup	Tank 1 Run	2 Setup	2 Run	3 Setup	3 Run	4 Setup	4 Run	5 Setup	5 Run	Totals Setup	Totals Run
Monday												
1200	4.0	7.6									4.0	7.6
1112			6.0	7.6	6.0	7.6	6.0	4.8	4.0	7.6	22.0	27.6
1450							3.5	2.8	3.5	7.6	29.0	38.0
Tuesday												
1450	3.5	7.6	3.5	2.0							7.0	9.6
1400			7.0	5.6	7.0	4.4					21.0	19.6
1310					4.0	3.2	4.0	7.6	3.5	7.6	33.0	38.0
Wednesday												
1310	4.0	7.6	4.0	7.6							8.0	15.2
1550					6.0	7.6	6.0	7.6	6.0	7.6	26.0	38.0
Thursday												
1550	6.0	7.2									6.0	7.2
1560			3.5	7.6	3.5	7.6	3.5	7.6	3.5	7.6	20.0	37.6
Friday												
1560	3.5	4.6									3.5	4.6
1600	3.5	3.0	3.5	7.6	3.5	7.6	3.5	7.6		2.6	21.0	34.0

In order to apply SIS, it is necessary to prepare daily work schedules making full use of the available tank time (capacity loading of the machines) and full use of the available manpower time (capacity loading of workers). We call this matching of capacity to load and load to capacity.

Table 6.5 provides all the information needed for an SIS schedule, if it is a true volume report. It is not useful, if it is only a schedule based on the industrial engineer's estimates. Estimates are not acceptable for SIS programs. It is necessary to determine reasonable expectancies by actual testing. In this case Table 6.5 is a volume report.

Directly from Table 6.6's last two columns we read 37.0 hours for setup and 189.0 hours for plating all the parts. Assuming full loading of tank capacity and 24 minutes of each day needed for cleaning the tanks, the required number of tanks and days are computed. Both setup times and plating times are different for each of the parts to be plated. The method to use is to combine data from different tanks (Table 6.6) that add up to or less than 7.6 hours of plating time. Another constraint is that, if the setup time for all the tanks used each day exceeds eight hours, additional setup men are needed. Also, setup time for each part is the same regardless of the quantity of parts being plated. The computation is shown in Table 6.7.

From this data, five tanks are needed. This number is based on using five platers. If it is thought desirable to reduce or increase the number of platers, then the number of tanks would change accordingly.

Assuming full capacity utilization, what is needed to complete the work? From the same data, five platers are needed for 4 days and only four on Friday. The number of setup mandays needed varies from 2.5 to 3.5.

Table 6.8 is the SIS schedule for Monday.

TABLE 6.8   SIS SCHEDULE

Part	R/E	Plater	Units To Be Plated	Scheduled Start	Scheduled Fin.	Act. Fin.	Diff.
1200	500	Elliott	3800	8:00	4:30		
1112	500	Jennings	3800	8:00	4:30		
1112	500	Brown	3800	8:00	4:30		
1112	500	Smith	2400	8:00	1:15		
1450	500	Smith	1400	1:15	4:30		
1450	500	Lee	3800	8:00	4:30		

While there is an increase in manpower (additional setup men) for this SIS schedule, the increase is more than offset by the need for only five tanks. As a result, there is a substantial saving in electrical power, supplies, maintenance, and an even greater gain in space that can be used for another operation.

CONNOLLY AIRCRAFT COMPANY

The Connolly Aircraft Company uses the following procedure in the production of hybrids (an assembly of integrated circuits and subminiature components):

The planner issues a work order which is placed in a plastic box for travel from one operation to the next in the production process. The box will contain the hybrid, a quality control form which lists each step in the process, schematics and blueprints, and a control sheet for indicating the next destination. The planner issues an overall schedule, which details the quantity to be made and the date required for delivery to stock. Each station in the process keeps an independent log of the pieces arrival and departure times. Operators at each station, on their time records, divide their total time (including overtime) among the various jobs they have worked on.

There is no record of the time the piece remains on the shelf, waiting for parts or inspection. Often this waiting time may take several days, and the actual time to install the part may be no more than fifteen minutes. Also test technicians may spend hours without work waiting for a quality control inspection to pass a repaired or assembled hybrid. This idle time is charged directly to the job and not to indirect accounts. As a result of this procedure, labor costs for the production of the hybrids is excessively high and, what is worse, the system does nothing to expedite the completion of the hybrids. In order to meet tight delivery schedules, an inordinate amount of overtime is used, often to no avail, because of a bottleneck in quality control inspection. Thousands of dollars wasted in this fashion are not visible in a program that is budgeted at many millions.

Analysis of the situation indicates that the assembly, inspection, and rework operations can not be greatly improved by introducing SIS. There is no wasted time. All operators are busy, and all production quotas are filled. There is no delay in reworking hybrids that fail in test. The real problem lies in the testing of the hybrids. This is because the flow of hybrids to and from testing is impeded by elaborate procedures and a multiplicity of handlings including planning, quality control inspection, storekeepers, customer inspectors, and supervisors.

The test operation does not lend itself as readily to the SIS technique as assembly. The establishment of work measures or productivity standards to the testing of a complex electronic module is extremely difficult.

While little improvement in the productivity of the assembly operation can be achieved by applying SIS, SIS will serve to pinpoint the real bottleneck in the production of hybrids—the steps between test and assembly. Even a small improvement in the assembly line may be worthwhile, because of more accurate assignment of labor costs to the various types of hybrids. This cost data may be important in pricing exercises during contract negotiations.

Suitable forms for SIS charts for the assembly area are:

Hybrid Assembly SIS Charts

Date _____

Hybrid	Assembler	Start	End	Number Completed	Units per hour

Date _____

Hybrid	Assembler	Number Completed	Time to Complete	R/E

Date _____

Hybrid	R/E	Assembler	No. Completed	Complet. Time Expect.	Diff.

Charts for the test stations will not be identical. The big difference is that a reasonable expectancy can not be determined for hybrid testing. The testing must use the supervisor's estimates as reasonable expectancies. The supervisor's estimates are based on his experience and knowledge. The only problem is that the tester may not be as experienced as the supervisor and, thus, may take some time to come up to the speed the supervisor expects. Also the unexpected in circuit faults

TABLE 6.9

Tester's Name	7:00	8:00	9:00	10:00	11:00	12:30	1:30	2:30	3:30	4:30
A. Slor	501	506		510				508		515
C. Conklin	502	504			505			503	507	
J. Swartz	601		602		603	606	607			610
W. Voss		701			702				703	
I. Douglas	801	803	804		807	810		815	802	805

The numbers on the time bars are hybrid serial numbers.

is always to be expected. Table 6.9 is a hybrid test schedule using the following data:

Five testers: A. Slor, C. Conklin, J. Swartz, W. Voss, and I. Douglas.

Hybrid Models	Estimated Time To Test
500 series	1 hour
600	2 hours
700	3 hours
800	0.75 hours

In Table 6.9, each drawn time bar starts as a job is assigned and is as long as the supervisor thinks it should take to test the hybrid. The supervisor has drawn an arrowhead to show when the job should be completed. If it is not completed at that time, he will extend the arrow to a new completion time, as has been done for hybrids 701, 702, and 703 being tested by W. Voss. When more than 20 minutes elapses before a new job starts, he makes a note of the reason. Reports on the causes of delay will serve to pinpoint problems so that action may be taken to correct them.

The schedule cannot be prepared in advance for the full day, because the estimates for test completion are only estimates. Because of the quality control inspection bottleneck, the flow of hybrids is not smooth and the number and type of hybrids available for test at any time is not predictable.

The use of such a schedule could document the reasons for low production output. We are reasonably sure that both assembly and test are not responsible for the problems. SIS schedules for both would prove that the bottleneck exists outside these areas. As with the assembly operation, an SIS schedule for test can fix the true costs for testing hybrids. Also with the SIS schedule the test supervisor, by tighter control, can quickly determine whether low output by a tester is due to the tester's incompetence or to unusual circuit troubles.

COX ELECTRONICS COMPANY

SIS can reduce delays in filling customer orders and, not only cut processing costs, but also convert inventory more rapidly to accounts receivable. The last benefit is so important today that it outweighs the cost reduction aspects. Three terms used in this application, need to be defined.

1. *Time in process* is total elapsed time from the receipt of an order to its shipment.
2. *In-process time* is that portion of the time in process when something is being done to or for the order.
3. *Waiting time* is an expensive item representing unproductive payroll costs as well as large delays in the filling of orders. Time in process is equal to the sum of in-process time and the waiting time.

Table 6.10 is the flow chart for orders received at the Cox Electronics Company up to their delivery to the production department.

TABLE 6.10   FLOW CHART FOR ORDERS AT COX ELECTRONICS COMPANY

Operation	Dept.	In-Process Time	Time In Process	Waiting Time
Open, stamp, sort	Mail	1 min.	1 hr.	59 min.
Deliver	Mail	5 min.	0.5 hr.	25 min.
Edit	Sales service	5 min.	2 hrs.	115 min.
Review	Sales manager	1 min.	1.25 hrs.	74 min.
Deliver	Mail	10 min.	1.5 hrs.	80 min.
Count	Office mgr.	0.5 min.	0.33 hrs.	19.5 min.
Type	Typing	10 min.	17 hrs.	16.66 hrs.
Deliver	Mail	5 min.	1 hr.	50 min.
Check	Sales service	5 min.	1.5 hrs.	85 min.
Deliver	Mail	5 min.	0.5 hr.	25 min.
Pick specs.	Engrg.	20 min.	19 hrs.	18.66 hrs.
Deliver	Mail	10 min.	2 hrs.	110 min.
Parts	Invent. Cont.	30 min.	5.5 hrs.	5 hrs.
Shop order	Produc. Plan.	2 hrs.	23.5 hrs.	21.5 hrs.
Pick parts	Stock	4 hrs.	24 hrs.	20 hrs.
Totals		7 hrs., 47.5 min.	100 hrs., 34.8 min.	92 hrs., 32.5 min.

We note that in-process time was only 7.7 percent of the time in process. In this case, time in process included the time the orders were in mail trays overnight. The time measurements were obtained by accompanying each order with a ticket on which arrival time at each station, operation start and stop, and departure time was recorded.

The best way to correct this problem was to attack the bottlenecks, the operations with the largest waiting times. A look at Table 6.10 would lead us to select the following as prime candidates for action:

Operation	Department	Waiting Time
Type	Typing	16.66 hrs.
Pick specs	Engrg.	18.66 hrs.
Shop order	Prod. Plan.	21.5 hrs.
Pick parts	Stock	20 hrs.

We know that in each of these cases the department in question had to hold the orders overnight, either because they could not complete them in time for the last mail, or because they did not receive the orders until late in the afternoon. We need to examine each day separately and, when the flow has been sufficiently expedited on a daily basis, to attempt to pull operations into the schedule of the previous day.

Large waiting times are the obvious bottlenecks, but the other operations should also be examined for possible savings. Computing the in-process time as a percentage of the time in process will reveal other candidates for action. For example:

First Day

Operation	Department	In-Process Time (% T. I. P.)	Waiting Time (mins.)
Open, stamp, sort	Mail	1.66	59
Deliver	Mail	16.8	25
Edit	Sales Serv.	4.1	115
Review	Sales mgr.	1.3	74
Deliver	Mail	11.1	80
Count	Office mgr.	2.5	19.5
Total			372.5

Note that the editing operation with 115 minutes of waiting time is an obvious target. On the other hand, the second mail delivery operation with 80 minutes of waiting time is not worth attention because the in-process time is 11.1 percent of the time in process. This may be reasonable, because of the length of the mail route. The review operation has 74 minutes waiting time and a 1.3% in-process time. One should look very carefully at the review operation. Other possibilities, even with fairly low waiting times, are the open, stamp and sort operation, and the count operation.

After analysis, the following corrections were made:

1. The mail department spends only 1 minute in opening, stamping, and sorting orders, but the orders are in the mail department for an hour. This is far too long. The supervisor found that the cause of this excessive waiting time was that the orders were mixed in with other mail and had to wait until all the mail was sorted. The waiting time was reduced by having a clerk pick mail that looked like orders first. Another clerk immediately opened, stamped, and sorted the orders.
2. A dramatic saving in waiting time was obtained for the editing operation by adding additional editors and by having the mail department sort the orders into types. The pre-sorting permitted the editors to quickly find orders that they could do best and fastest.
3. Waiting time for review of orders was high chiefly because the flow of orders to the sales manager happened in spurts. Reduction of the editing waiting time allowed a smoother flow of orders.

After the corrections, the first day flow should look like Table 6.11.

We now approach the second day, and reduce the time in process for as many operations as possible. Then we shift three hours of the second day's time in process to the first day. The second day's savings,

TABLE 6.11   FIRST DAY FLOW CHART

Operation	Department	In-Process Time (% T. I. P.)	Waiting Time (mins.)
Open, stamp, sort	Mail	3.3	29.0
Deliver	Mail	16.7	25.0
Edit	Sales serv.	16.6	25.0
Review	Sales mgr.	6.6	14.0
Deliver	Mail	11.1	80.0
Count	Office mgr.	2.5	19.5
Total			192.5

Saving: 180 mins. or 3 hrs.

plus the three hours saved the first day, is the amount of time in process that can be shifted from the third day to the second day. Where orders normally took a week to be processed, they now can be processed in three days. Not only that, but also the number of clerks needed to do the processing can be reduced by using SIS, resulting in dollar savings in addition to a time saving. The time saving is particularly important when customers request deliveries within two or three weeks. Even two days lost can create a serious problem for production.

SIS requires all departments to plan their work and check the progress of the work at short intervals. This tight control makes it possible to predict and to avoid delays by taking the proper action. SIS can guarantee that the shortest time in process will be employed, thus, enabling quicker delivery than the competition, which in turn, will bring in more business.

Applying SIS brings to the surface the many areas in the company where full time employees are used to fill part time jobs, jobs in which the work requirements are not sufficient to fill a full day. The employee hired for such a job is usually not trained to do anything else. As Parkinson's law points out, work seems to expand to fill the time available for its completion. By establishing reasonable expectancies of performance, SIS uncovers such work stretchouts.

Reducing waiting times converts full time jobs to part time jobs. The best solution here is not to employ single skill, part-time workers but to employ multiskilled, full-time people to handle two or more part time jobs. It is important to know which employees can do other jobs and to tailor new hirings to the exact needs of the company. For example, one would not hire a full time drill press operator who can not operate any other machine if only 25% of the production in-process time involves the use of the drill press.

Among the synergistic benefits from SIS is synchronization of the activities required to fill an order to the delivery schedule. Planning has made it possible to anticipate all delays. Customer complaints are minimized, and the sales department benefits. Less clerical manpower is needed, and the morale of the workforce is raised.

In the Cox Electronics Company we observed that, with SIS, the processing of orders was reduced from five days to three days. This saving would be for naught if the filling of the order was overly delayed. From Table 6.10 we can prepare a table for order filling. We omit mail department operations, because we assume that little or no savings can be realized in that area.

Note that Table 6.10 does not include production, test and inspection, packing, and shipping. These would make another interesting problem. The total in-process time is, from Table 6.10, 7 hours and

TABLE 6.12   ORDER FILLING FLOW CHART

Operation	Department	In-Process Time (% T. I. P.)	Waiting Time (mins.)
Pick specs.	Engrg.	1.8	1120
Parts inv.	Inv. Control	10.8	300
Shop order	Prod. Plan.	9.3	1290
Pick parts	Stock	20.0	1200
Total			3910

47.5 minutes. The total waiting time, from Table 6.12, is 3910 minutes or 65.16 hours. Thus, the total in-process time is 10.6 percent of the time in process.

Addenda:

1. Approximately 50% reduction in waiting time would be a reasonable goal.
2. Picking specifications with a low 1.8 percent in-process time should permit the largest savings in waiting time; picking parts, with 20 percent in-process time, the smallest. Another consideration is the departments involved. Engineering, inventory control, and production planning are bound to be well organized and require minimum time to process orders. Therefore, waiting time can be expected to be readily minimized, since it is probably due to problems with other departments. Parts picking, on the other hand, is a time consuming process and the waiting time is probably unavoidable for that reason.
3. Cutting waiting times in proportion to the value of in-process time, Table 6.13 is computed with new waiting times giving the total saving in time.

TABLE 6.13   WAITING TIME TABLE

Operation	Department	In-Process Time As % Time In Process	Waiting Time (mins.)
Pick specs.	Engrg.	20.0	80.0
Parts inv.	Inv. Contr.	20.0	120.0
Shop order	Prod. Plan.	20.0	440.0
Pick parts	Stock	24.0	760.0
Total			1400.0

Saving = 2510 minutes or 41 hours, 50 minutes

TABLE 6.14   WAITING TIME COMPUTATIONS

Operation	Assumed % Time In Process	In-Process Time (mins.)	New Time In Proc. (mins.)	New Waiting Time (mins.)
Pick specs.	20	20	100	80
Parts inv.	20	30	150	120
Shop order	20	120	600	440
Pick parts	24	240	1000	760

This table required higher goals for in-process time. The methods used to compute this table shown in Table 6.14.

Sample computation: New time in-process = 20/0.2 = 100 minutes.

100 − 20 = 80 min = new waiting time

This saving is probably unrealistic but will serve to demonstrate the method and what it can do for customer service.

4. Combining the saving for this operation with that for the order processing gives a new total time saved in customer service. Three hours were saved for order processing in previous computation. In this computation, 41 hours, 50 minutes are saved. This is more than one week cut from the time to fill orders. Even assuming this saving is not achievable, it is proof that the two day reduction can be achieved very easily.

THE KMC TOOL AND DIE COMPANY

The KMC Tool and Die Company had 100 identical machines in its main plant. The deterioration and failure characteristics of each machine for any time period (between inspections) was determined by past experience and shown in Table 6.15.

TABLE 6.15   MACHINE FAILURE CHARACTERISTICS

| Initial Condition | Probability At End Of Period | | |
	Good	Deteriorated	Failed
Good	.90	.09	.01
Deteriorated	.0	.90	.10
Failed	1.0	.0	.0

On the basis of past experience with such machines:

Average Inspection & Repair Times	Costs
(W_1) Preventive inspection = 0.2 manhours	(C_0) Setup = \$5,000
(W_2) Preventive repair = 1.0 manhour	(C_M) Manyear = 10,000
(D) Emergency diagnosis/repair = 4.0 hr.	(C_D) downtime = \$500

From the same experience with the machines, Figure 29 was plotted for the failure characteristics. Failures can be traded for preventive repairs or vice versa by increasing or decreasing the time between inspections. The optimum choice depends on the relative marginal costs. These costs are plotted in Figure 30 as a function of the number of maintenance men.

Figure 31 is based on the following computations:

1. From Figure 30, two-man crew marginal cost for inspection is \$45. Cost of preventive repair is \$360.
2. From Figure 29, one month between inspections has an expected number per year of 2.7 for preventive repairs, 0.18 for failures.
3. For two maintenance men and one month between inspections, cost of failures = DC_D = 4.0 × \$500 = \$2000.
4. Total annual cost = inspection marginal cost × number of inspections + cost of preventive repairs × expected number per year + failure costs × expected number per year = \$45 × 12 + \$360 × 2.7 + \$2000 × 0.18 = \$1872.

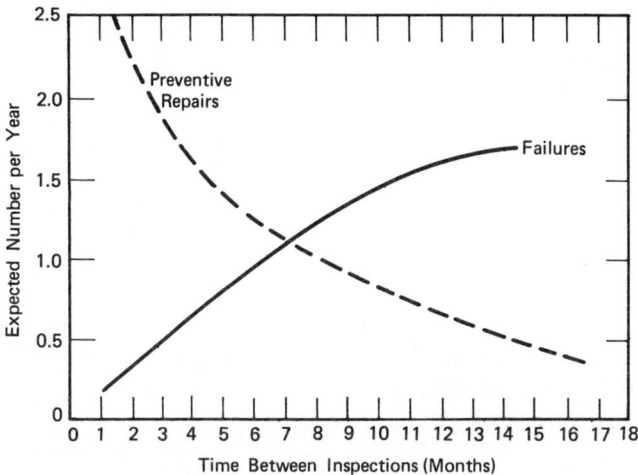

Figure 29   Expected Number of Repairs

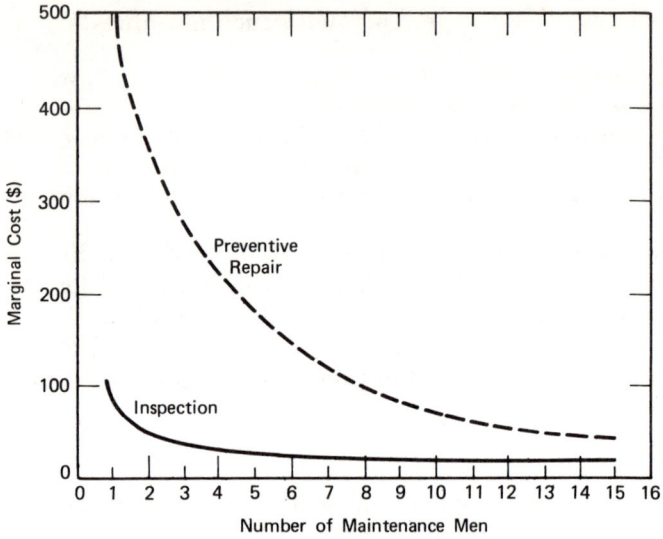

Figure 30   Marginal Cost of Maintenance

The following values are computed:

Crew Size	Time Betw. Inspects. (Mos.)	Annual Costs ($)
One man	1	2910
	2	2225
	4	2600
	6	2600
Two men	1	1872
	2	1580
	4	2183
	6	2322
Four men	1	1254
	2	1145
	4	1871
	6	2114

For the three cases plotted, minimum costs coincide with inspections at different intervals. Then,

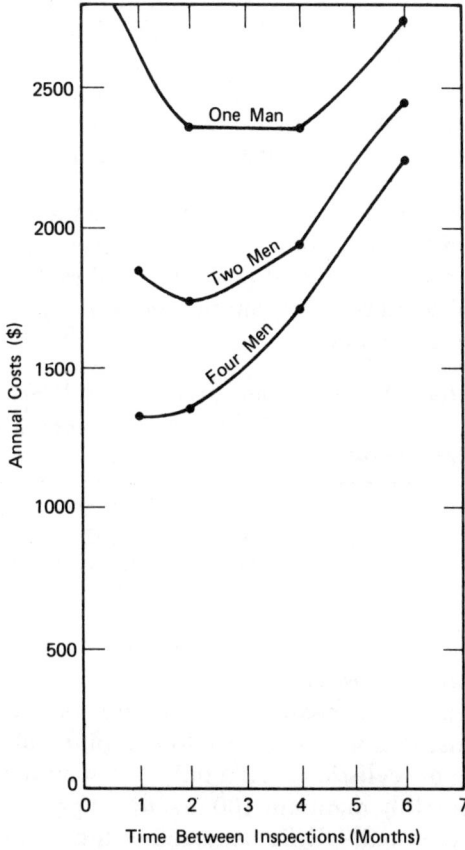

Figure 31   Annual Marginal Costs of Maintenance

Number of Men	Min. Cost Inspect. Intervals
One	2 to 4 months
Two	2 months
Four	1 month

Total maintenance costs for each of these minimum inspection intervals are computed as follows:

1-Month Interval	One Man	Total Costs ($) Two Men	Four Men
Total costs	291,000	187,200	131,400
Setup costs	60,000	60,000	60,000
Manpower costs	10,000	20,000	40,000
Totals	361,000	267,200	231,400

This table indicates that the minimum cost for a one-month inspection interval results from using a four man crew. The final decision must be based on computing all possible combinations.

The total costs for all possible combinations of crew size and inspection intervals are computed:

Total Annual Maintenance Costs ($1000)

Months Interval	Number of Maintenance Men One	Two	Four
1	361	267.2	231.4
2	306	252.2	232.4
4	306	277.1	270.2
6	342.5	324	323.5

From this table, the optimum choice is a four-man crew with twelve inspections a year. In most cases, the optimum may not be an obvious choice, and it may be necessary to compute for intervals of weeks instead of months. It is not necessary to compute values for one-man crews, since it is unrealistic to have only one maintenance man. One man could not possibly maintain 100 machines properly. What would happen if more than one failure occurred at the same time?

CHAPTER 7

PLANNING AND ORGANIZING DCR PROGRAMS

The process of organizing a firm combines a complex of men, materials, machines, and other resources into a business enterprise that will hopefully be profitable. Organizing for an effective DCR program must not be a temporary measure, else the improvements will vanish with time. Productivity improvement involves making an existing organization operate as efficiently *as possible*. DCR calls for changing the organization and its objectives, if it is necessary to achieve profitability, but these changes are usually minor. Where productivity accepts the limitations of a specific situation, profitability demands rejection of the situation and adoption of a new organization.

COMPANY ORGANIZATION (1,2,3,4)

Organization has been defined as the pattern of ways in which large numbers of people, engaged in a complexity of tasks, relate themselves to each other in the accomplishment of mutually agreed purposes. The purpose of the company is to make a profit. The purposes of the individuals in the company are not necessarily the same as the company. Engineers and scientists rarely concern themselves with profits. In fact, they usually participate in profit-related decisions only to resolve engineering problems in the products. Marketing specialists have only one purpose, sales volume. They, too, are only called upon when sales volume or market choices affect the profits. The factory's concern with productivity, as we have seen, may be only remotely related to profit.

What is supposed to be an integration of activities with a single purpose is in reality an heterogeneous organization with a multiplicity of purposes. It becomes a large task for top management in large companies to keep the "herd" on the narrow trail to profitability. In small companies, where top management wears the many hats of department heads, objective decisions are rarely made. The company goal is more likely to be suppressed in favor of the department goal.

The enormity of the problem becomes evident from an examination of the research into the *span of management.* This concept relates to the number of subordinates a superior can supervise effectively. In an American Management Association survey of 100 large companies, it was found that the number of executives reporting to the presidents were from one to 24. The median number was nine. In 41 small companies, the median was eight.

Dealing with the productivity concept, a large span has advantages. The Sears Roebuck Company, for example, found that managers with a large number of subordinates were forced to delegate authority. The subordinates were then able to make important decisions. The question arises: are these decisions furthering department goals or company goals?

Research on the relative advantages and disadvantages of tall and flat company organizations has not been decisive. Different sizes of companies and different industries, have requirements that make some particular forms of organization preferable to others. The revamping of an existing organization must be approached with caution. Both individuals and groups within an organization will resist change that threatens their status, security, or other need satisfactions. There must be sound economic reasons for the change as well as solid evidence that a high probability of success exists. Since there is no weight of evidence to support a general preference for one type of organization over another, the only changes in company organization that can be recommended for DCR must be of a *relative minor nature.*

The change, if needed, must be in department goals and in the degree of department participation in company planning and DCR decisions. Whatever the mode of organization, usually units of the organization are relatively independent. Each sets its own goals and makes its own plans. Management then fits the individual plans into its master plan. The preferred scheme is a team effort for planning and goal setting. This arrangement is best for nonDCR firms as well, because all units understand the reasons for the goals set by a management team rather than the unit manager. The largest advantage is the shortening of communication links.

A department manager, in the process of planning, must translate company policy into terms of his department's operations. His interpretation is biased by his desire to maintain the status quo and by

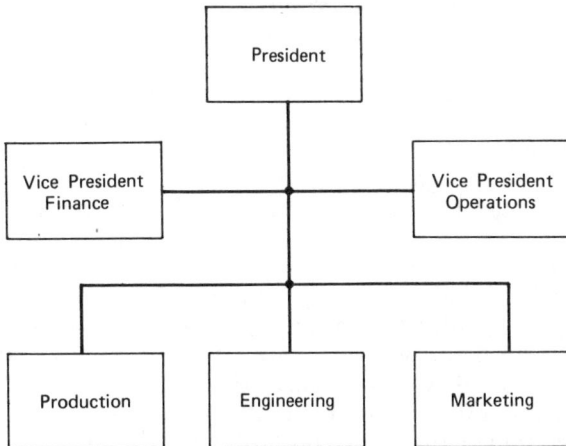

Figure 32   Juniper Company Organization Chart

his striving to "look good" and avoid failures. As a member of a planning team, there is no need for translation. He is getting a reading directly from the fountainhead. He sees, too, the interdependence of the actions of all the units of the company.

Example: The Juniper Company organization is shown in Figure 32.

The vice president of operations, George Adams, was responsible for the planning. He used forecasts prepared by the marketing manager and earnings reports from the finance vice president. Adams would then provide engineering with a budget and request a completion schedule in return. Production would be given projections of demand and asked to supply a plan for that department. The master plan would be developed from the data supplied by these three units.

Marketing's forecasts are based on Juniper's goals—product line, markets, share of markets, growth, and the like. Engineering's data merely specifies when new products will be ready for production if given X dollars, and, also, the cost of engineering support to production and marketing. Production's goals are manufacturing sufficient products to meet the anticipated demand at the lowest possible cost. The data production supplies will consist of manpower schedules, purchasing requirements, and unit costs.

Observe that engineering's goal is to complete designs within a time and dollar schedule. A submerged goal of using all the budgeted funds exists. There is no compulsion to avoid overruns because engineering is mysterious and unpredictable to nonengineers and delays and high costs are accepted as a necessary evil. Such overruns and delays may seriously affect company plans. In any case, the point is that engineering's goals are not the same as the company's.

Production is no better than engineering in the matter of goals. Productivity is the goal and productivity is related to company goals only in the matters of quantity and manufacturing cost of the products. In achieving the productivity goal, there may be excessive engineering, inventory, and both direct and indirect labor costs. The end result may be that the unit cost may be too high to permit Juniper to capture its goal-share of the market.

Juniper Company was fortunate. While it rarely met or surpassed its goals, it was profitable. However, if a DCR program was to be initiated, it would have little chance of success without a reorganization. A planning committee would need to be formed with George Adams as chairman. The committee members would include the finance vice president, production manager, engineering manager, and the marketing manager.

With the committee in operation, the feasibility of company goals can be determined quickly and reasonably. Achievable goals for the three departments can be developed. The department goals will reflect the interdependency of the three units and will be subsets of the company goals. That is, the master plan will be built from the top down rather than from the bottom up. As a result, there should be a minimum of failures.

The reorganization suggested for the Juniper Company is not realizable with larger and more complex companies. The objective of the reorganization is to permit the formation of a planning committee. The committee needs to be composed of managers of the major elements of a *profit center*. A profit center is a subdivision of a large company and is concerned with a single product. For example, an electronics company might have a consumer electronics division and an industrial electronics division. Each of these divisions can be treated as profit centers. Each normally has its own specialized departments, marketing, production, engineering, and the like. If they do not, it is recommended that they be so organized before attempting a DCR program. Then each can form its own planning committee.

PROGRAM ORGANIZATION

Formation of the planning committee is only a first step in organizing for a DCR program. It is also necessary to provide the committee with the necessary skills for development of the plan. Elsewhere in the company, changes will be needed to install SIS and switch from the productivity approach to that of profitability.

There is a strong temptation to rely heavily on outside consultants for most cost reduction programs. This is self-defeating, because those responsible for administering the program do not have this assistance when they need it most—when the program is far down the road and the problems begin to appear. Admittedly consultants can do fine work, and an outside viewpoint is invaluable. However, it is imperative that every member of the management team thoroughly understand how and why the plan is being developed if the program is to be effective throughout its life.

There is a need for consultants to assist in the formative stage of the program. The consultant can provide guidance and direction but should not take an active role. When the program calls for special skills, such as industrial engineering or short interval scheduling, the manager may need to call on consultants if his department is deficient in these skills. Since DCR permits fairly sharp definitions of the improvements needed, the manager can order exactly the amount of consultant services he requires. There is no need for feasibility studies or all out studies.

The company organization changes required for a DCR program are as follows:

1. Membership on the planning committee of either an internal or external accountant with skills in sensitivity analysis, cost analysis and accounting, capital expenditure analysis, and return on investment analysis.
2. Reporting charges. All charges for labor, materials, and the like, are not to be against general accounts, such as machine shop or tool crib. Charges are to be made to specific jobs.
3. Some companies have quality assurance, industrial engineering, and similar operations subelements reporting directly to the president or division manager. The organization should be revised. For example, industrial engineering costs are chiefly direct costs of production. The industrial engineering director should, therefore, report to the manufacturing manager. Any industrial engineering work in other areas would be charged to those areas and not to production. The intent here is to accurately determine the costs for any area of the company and avoid omitting items such as industrial engineering. In most cases, industrial engineering ends up as a fixed cost of the overall company operations. The same principle applies to other departments such as industrial relations.

COMPANY PLANNING (5)

Planning should not be confused with forecasting. The latter is an attempt to find the most probable course of events or a range of probabilities. Planning is deciding what one will do about them. A business plan states the results that are to be achieved and indicates what the people in the organization can and should do to achieve them. There are three kinds of business planning:

1. For current business.
2. For continuing in business.
3. For development and growth.

Planning with DCR does not change this or the procedures to be followed except in the matter of goals.

Planning should proceed along a specific path.

1. The company must gather information on the external environment to determine the organization's needs. The external environment includes the broad social, cultural, political, and economic parameters in which the business must operate. All of these parameters, affecting the long range plans of the firm, must be considered if the plan is to be successful in achieving its goals. They are less critical for short term plans. Note that DCR, while useful in short term plans, is most effective with long term planning.

   Because it is difficult to obtain knowledge of competitive long term plans, the competitive environment is more important to short term planning. The competitive environment covers the industry in which the firm is involved, the relationship with competitors, and the relationship with customers. Marketing intelligence is extremely important to survival in the free enterprise system. The quality of the marketing intelligence must be high for the DCR program to succeed.

   Example: What follows was a memorandum explaining market analyses used in a 5-year plan for a medium-sized aerospace company. The plan was successful in obtaining about $3 million in new business for the company.
   Subject: Explanation of market analyses in 5-year plan.
   Objectives:

   1. Sales goals with high credibility.
   2. Reduction of sales territories to those offering the greatest potential for company products.

3. Finding weaknesses and gaps in market intelligence.
4. Forcing a better understanding of potential customers.
5. Attempting to introduce the consideration of optimality into marketing decisions.
6. Reinforcing decisions based on judgment (by mapping the logic used).

Justification for quantitative analysis: It has been proven experimentally by the Air Force that better decisions are made if the decision maker makes microscopic judgments instead of macroscopic ones. That is, the human mind cannot compute as fast and as accurately as a machine, when a multiplicity of data inputs exist. In the Air Force experiments, human "seat-of-the-pants" decisions on fire control and on mission deployments were in both cases more often in error than the decisions made by a computer, *even though the data to the computer was unreliable.* We have a similar situation here where each marketing opportunity needs to be evaluated on 10–15 criteria. Even if the data for evaluation on these criteria have low credibility and even if the weighting of the criteria is arbitrary, the integrated scores for all the parameters will be *closer* to the truth than any snap judgment based on only one or two at the best. It should be noted that in no sense is this anymore than a *computed hunch,* the computed hunch has a greater reliability than the uncomputed hunch.

Steps in the analysis:

1. Reduce the number of targets for new business to make for a reasonable size of the problem. Even with omission of markets where the potential is for followon only, we have a total of 20 possible targets. Screening could be done by uncomputed hunch, but there are a total of 17 criteria by which to judge each opportunity. Qualitative data is quantified by evaluation on a scale of 10. For example, if we have good relations with the customer, that market would have a customer relations value of 7.5. If the value is exceptionally good, 9 or 10. The scores for each marketing target are computed in the following manner:

   x = dollar considerations = budget + 2 × company investment + 3 = software volume + average contract value.

   y = corporate objectives = geographic location + kind of work + corporate goals + 2 × degree of fit + 2 × timing + growth potential + 2 × type of contracts + political problems.

z = environment = 3 × probability of success + 2 × competition + customer relations + available resource + 2 × previous contracts.

$$x^2y^2z^2 = \text{Score}$$

Numbers are squared to double spread between scores. Twelve targets were chosen in this manner. To this was added a miscellaneous opportunity to cover fortuitous business. This also included a number of previously rejected targets. The targets selected were those for which marketing needed to be planned. Their scores were a clue to the type of plan required.

2. For each of the 13 marketing opportunities, estimates are obtained of their FY69 potential in dollars. Estimates are also made on the probability of success for achieving this potential. This is done for 25 company products previously identified. Multiplying the potential and the probability of success for each target for each product gives marketing's value in its attempt to sell the particular product to a specific market. The sum of these values for a single market is the expectation for that market and can be used as a sales goal. However, the larger values are the ones that would be most fruitful. One might select only these for inclusion in the total expectation of the target.

3. Market intelligence sheets are prepared for each of the 13 opportunities. These have the following information.

Description and location
    Potential
Highest expectation products
    Most recent budget figures
    Software dollar volume
    Average size of contracts
    Capability fit
    Legal and political problems
    Competition
        Name, size of current contract, customer relations, duration of contract
    Company marketing
        Previous investment, customer relations, resource availability, summary of contacts, names of important contacts

4. Plot potential curves for each market as in Figure 33. Point A is the expected value obtained in step 2. This is made the end

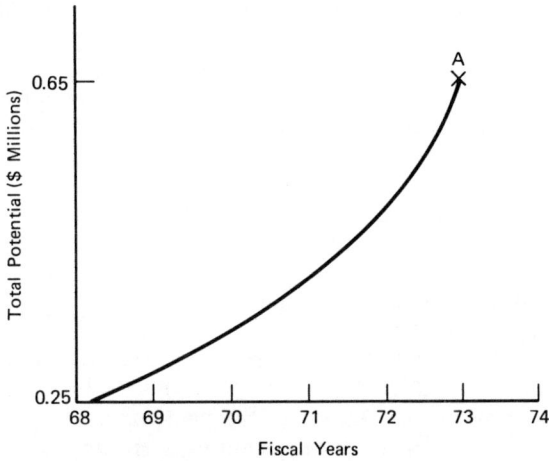

Figure 33   Sample Marketing Potential Curve

goal for the 5-year plan. The initial point on the curve is the sales goal for FY68 as it appeared in the program plan. The shape of the curve is selected intuitively. Succeeding program plans will be able to modify the curve as progress is noted. These curves will serve as control measures for the effectiveness of the marketing and the planning.

5. Goals preparation. The goals for each of the 5 years in the plan are obtained by summing the values picked for the specific fiscal year. The markets for which this is to be done would be those rated as most important in step 1 and those additional markets that the marketing staff has the time to market effectively.

2. During planning the company must gather information on the internal environment. The internal organization's strengths, skills, specializations, and development are the skeleton on which the planning is hung. Often the company is not aware of capabilities that could have an important bearing on the profitability. The aerospace company in a previous example was totally unaware of a cadre of engineers and scientists with skills in communications research and development. This capability was demonstrated by tabulating and abstracting the technical papers published by the engineering staff. Not only was the number of papers extremely large, but also the contents were innovative and, more important, matched many of the customer requirements.

3. Planning includes identification and study of the factors limiting the organization's profitability and growth in the future.

4. Objectives or goals of the business must be established. There is, first, the overriding objective of obtaining the maximum return on the company investment. DCR adds the requirement that the return be large enough to permit substantial reinvestment and an increase in the net worth. Secondary objectives will vary as widely as the number of industries and businesses. A startup business plan seeking financing will have goals that are wanted by that type of investors. Banks and insurance companies might look for security for their funds, conservative management and a product that assures profitability. Venture capitalists are more concerned with growth in terms of sales volume. Public investors want good price-earnings ratios for the shares. A plan for a hospital might have as its main objective, expansion of its facilities. The hospital would have for its DCR objective large enough grants and donations beyond operating expenses to permit a new building and/or new equipment.

5. All alternatives must be analyzed. DCR programs using data collected for that purpose should analyze all possible alternatives, such as continuation of current products at various volume levels, revision of current products, development of new products and new markets, switches in industries, mergers, and acquisitions. A figure of merit would be assigned to each alternative much as was done in the example. The figure of merit best used for DCR is the profitability index. The alternatives from which choice(s) are to be made would have the largest profitability indices. The current operations are thus evaluated and improvements or replacements readily determined.

6. The best alternatives should be selected. The alternatives with the highest profitability indices are now compared with the inventory of company resources and capabilities. Alternatives with the best match are prime candidates. Final screening consists of determining which alternative best meets company objectives. If more than one alternative emerges after this selection procedure, then the final decision must be made by the president of the company or the chairman of the board.

7. The company must determine actions to achieve the objectives. Obviously, this can be as simple as reducing operating costs or as complex as changing the distribution system. The only requirement for this activity is to arrive at actions that are reasonable and feasible within the time scale of the plan. It may be necessary to obtain expert opinions from outside consultants.

8. A time schedule for the actions must be developed. At this point, each department with representation on the planning committee

must not only contribute estimates, but also must approve the master schedule. That is, all departments must be aware of their roles in the master plan and of their interdependence with the others. All concerned must know exactly how they fit into the plan. Each department's objectives are now synchronized with the company objectives.

9. Prepare the master plan. The master plan can now be written. It will consist of background material gathered in the first four steps of the procedure, a brief description of all of the alternatives and their ratings, reasons for selecting alternatives, a detailed description of the alternative chosen, forecasts or estimates of the results expected, the actions needed to achieve the objectives, and the time schedule for the actions.

Example: For very long-term plans, the profitability index may not be a sufficient figure of merit for comparing alternatives. As an example of such a case, consider the Ajax Manufacturing Company's dilemma in planning the manufacture of a new product. The president feels that he needs ten years to recover the costs of a new plant.

His three officers presented him with three estimates of future markets, prices, labor costs, material costs, plant utilization, labor efficiency, taxes, and the like. Each of the three men had different backgrounds which gave them different slants on the various factors of the problem. Figure 34 plots the three profit estimates.

In the early years, the forecasts were fairly close together since the officers felt more certain of near term than of long term results. As the planning period was extended, greater uncertainty

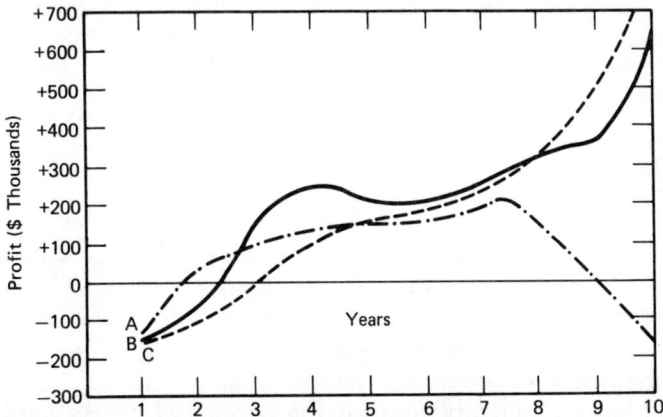

Figure 34   Ajax Mfg. Co. Profit Forecasts

about some of the factors tended to make the estimates of profit vary from a very large gain for two of the curves to a loss for the third. The number of forecasts available would probably vary directly as the number of forecasters with alternative inputs from which to choose.

No elaborate techniques are required for selecting an alternative for a short term plan since the error derived from an incorrect choice is not significant.

The 5-year forecasts of airline traffic made by three independent forecasters in one year were not only identical, but also were precisely correct. The reliability for longer periods of time can not be expected to be as high. The selection of the correct long term alternative is just as important to the short term plans as it is to the long term plans, because they are very much dependent on each other.

Observe that if the short term plan is based on forecast A and the long term on forecast C of Figure 34, a very wide discrepancy exists at the end of the second year. This is interpreted in this manner: if forecast A is correct, then the long term plan will be over-compensating at the end of the second year, because of the expectation of a large loss at that time. If forecast C is correct, then the short term plan will have no cushion to meet the predicted losses. The solution is to select a single forecast for both the short and the long term plans.

The problem, in this case, for the DCR program is that we are seeking consistent high profitability over the entire ten years. Forecast A shows decreasing profits after the seventh year. Alternative A is acceptable only if it is feasible to switch to one of the others at that time. The point of this is that the DCR plan must be projected throughout the entire long term period and must include contingency plans for expected or unexpected downtrends or changes in the economy. In a DCR program this can be built into the cost standards. Conventional productivity plans cannot provide for contingencies.

Action Plans

Figure 35 is a typical action plan, in this case, the marketing plan for an aerospace firm. A, B, C, D, and E are all products or programs.

Specific customer programs are identified in Step 1. The total resources or capability required for success in this market is listed in terms of specific accomplishments. This is helpful when preparing proposals, since, if the company does become a contender in this market, it will be able to readily outline the reasons why it is. The specific key accomplishments may be in the form of past projects successfully

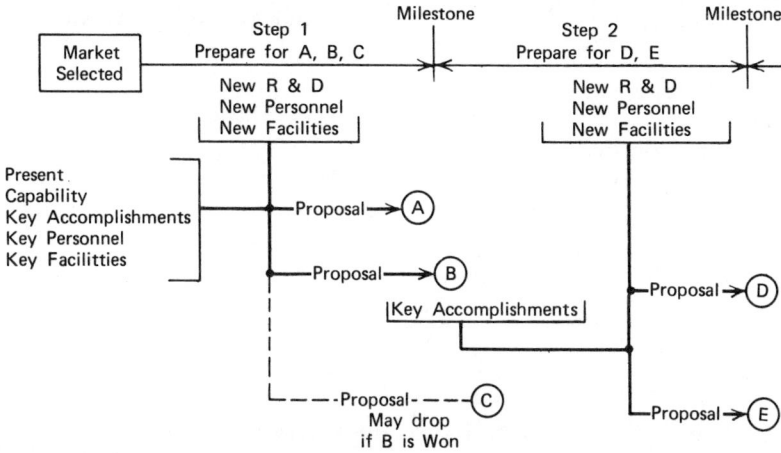

Figure 35 Typical Action Plan

completed, R&D performed, personnel, facilities, manufacturing know-how, good will, location, reputation, supply lines, and the like. The difference between the total resources required and that capability already in-house will provide a measure of the new resources that must be acquired.

Supporting research and development programs need to be scheduled and controlled to achieve the new product. Other requirements such as improving old products, reducing production costs, hiring new scientific skills, and increasing basic research may be needed. An important part of bolstering capability is production planning which would include the integration of new equipment, scheduling, new quality and inspection methods. Even the entry into the market requires detailed marketing plans covering new selling efforts, reorganization of sales force, pricing, and market intelligence. Organizational changes may be needed as a result of the planning. The R&D and production inputs must be funded and these financial plans require preparation of new equity financing or borrowing, budgeting of capital, and detailed financial forecasts.

In Step 2, the firm is preparing for product D and E in the same market or for the same customer. The key accomplishments applicable here are expected to result from contract participation for products A, B, and C, and this is done for succeeding Steps. Because the risks are greater as resources are allocated toward projects further in the future, the R&D applicable to later Steps is kept small relative to that for Step 1.

The detailing of each Step is a short range plan. The overall action plan is a long range one. Detailed action plans are generated for one Step at a time. In this way, the meshing of short range activities to meet long range plans is facilitated. The specific action plans for R&D, such as production and finance, need to be developed simultaneously and in parallel by the responsible organization. Good communications between planners is then necessary to ensure that conflicts are avoided and compatibility ensured.

In summary, a well-conceived action plan covers all the actions that are necessary to achieve the objectives of a plan. It details who should do what and when.

The basic stages are:

1. Divide into steps the activities necessary to achieve the objective.
2. Note the relations between each of the steps, especially any necessary sequences, the order in which they are to be taken.
3. Decide who is to be responsible for performing each step.
4. Determine the resources that will be needed for each step.
5. Estimate the time required for each step.
6. Assign definite dates for each part, the milestones.

PROGRAM PLANNING

We have indicated how DCR affected the company planning. Planning of the DCR program itself is not very different from planning any cost reduction program, except that DCR may have a multiplicity of cost standards. In addition, the DCR planning requires an action plan with contingency plans. The DCR master plan, since it is a long term plan, will specify a time or contingency schedule for the standards. For example, the master plan might have a schedule such as this:

Date	P.I.	Unit Cost
June, 1977	0.8 or higher	$5.45
June, 1977	0.6 to 0.7	5.00
June, 1977	less than 0.5	Drop product

Because, unlike productivity programs, DCR is not limited to industrial engineering for cost reduction, action plans must be provided as guidance in implementing the plan. The three contingencies in our example might have the following action plans:

Contingency	Action
A	None
B	Increase factory productivity 9%
C	Switch to Model 937

The last contingency action is, obviously, not something that can be accomplished overnight. The action plan should include a detailed plan for this switch. The action plan should pin point the indicator to be used to signal the start up of the new model. The signal should be given sufficiently early to permit an orderly changeover. Also, the plan needs to indicate actions to be taken by purchasing, inventory, sales, maintenance, personnel, and so forth.

Example: Market research for five products was analyzed quantitatively, resulting in the following data:

	Dollar Considerations X	Corporate Objectives Y	Environment Z
Product A	5	8	5
B	6	4	7
C	3	8	9
D	7	5	4
E	8	3	4

The figure-of-merit formula is $X^2Y^2Z^2$.

Figures of merit for the five products were calculated as follows:

A 114
B 101
C 154
D 90
E 89

C is definitely the preferred product. We should not make quick decisions on the others. Consider the percent differences:

	% Down From C
C	—
A	25
B	34
D	41
E	42

The worst one, E, is only 42% down from C. Remember that the scores are arbitrary figures of merit to be used only for comparing the products. The scores are too close to make any specific product undesirable. Further research is needed. If new data does not resolve this problem, then probably all five products merit acceptance.

PLANNING CASE STUDY: SATURN X PROJECT

Jet Power, Inc., is a company that has concentrated on making jet and rocket engines for aircraft and space vehicles. It has enjoyed a measure of success attributed to its dynamic founder and president, Jonathan Winthrop. He made a name for himself in the pioneer period of commercial aviation as an aeronautical engineer with revolutionary engine designs. As a result, Winthrop was not only well known in the aerospace industry but also knew everyone of importance by their first name. Everyone of importance meant many that were highly placed in both NASA and Air Force management. This was to be expected since most of the leaders in aerospace came from the ranks of the aircraft manufacturers.

Winthrop was not averse to taking advantage of his contacts to obtain marketing intelligence—chiefly of forthcoming needs—which helped Jet Power obtain a virtual monopoly in the field of small and medium sized engines. Jet Power's success could not be attributed entirely to Winthrop's personal marketing. A considerable part of it sprang from his enthusiasm for science and research.

The Jet Power laboratories held scores of patents on devices for the improvement of space propulsion engines. It had done well because it restricted its efforts to a very narrow range of size and power in engines and under the leadership of Dr. Wittenberg, a world-famous authority, had gained an enviable reputation for highly efficient, reliable engines that were sought for aircraft and the smaller, unmanned space vehicles.

The company had grown in a decade to a multi-plant giant employing 10,000 with annual sales of close to $200 million. Its profit margin, typical for companies dealing with the government, had been a rather low 4% and its ratio of net income after taxes to book value of assets had been in the range of 7–10%. The company's credit rating was excellent, and its cash reserve small but adequate.

The growth rate had been phenomenal in the early years, thanks to Winthrop's foresight in hiring an assistant whose chief function was planning and who had a good background in management science techniques. The decisions made in the past had always been right. The most recent growth rates, however, had dropped to about 5%. This might have been due to a leveling off both in the company's desire to grow and in the growth of the aerospace industry. The swing in government spending toward the solution of internal socio-economic problems had hurt the industry.

Jet Power's annual report for 1969 gave the following fitures:

Sales	$200 million
Expenses	184 million
Net	16 million
Net Worth	$400 million

It was at a board meeting shortly after his return from a professional society meeting on space missions of the future that Winthrop presented a new proposal. He wanted Jet Power to enter the field of large booster rockets, the monsters that can loft huge manned vehicles into space. NASA was already developing the Saturn for the Apollo program, but surely, Winthrop reasoned, NASA would be receptive to a newer and larger booster, particularly if it had all the reliability and efficiency for which Jet Power was noted. Winthrop called the proposed program the Saturn X project.

The project planning vice president, Al Jennings, pointed out that the company's engineers were past masters at every phase of the smaller engine technology. He said that Dr. Wittenberg was certainly the best R&D leader in the field. But the company was pretty well removed from the details of new product development, Jennings said, especially new products which were very much different from the ones they had dealt with previously. In addition the new, younger engineers had been trained to take the place of the more experienced men and, therefore, had no new skills to offer. It would be necessary to install a rigorous retraining program for the R&D staff. It was obvious that Dr. Wittenberg would either have to be replaced or a second laboratory set up for the large engines and their fuels.

Not only would all this be an affront to the engineering department's pride, but also there would be a time lag between the learning process and effective application of the new knowledge. In addition, production, test, and fuel storage facilities would have to be expanded or new ones built. Shipping the huge engines would be a major problem, because of the vehicles to be used and the distances over which they might have to be transported. It might be necessary to set up new plants closer to Cape Kennedy to mitigate this problem.

All of this Jennings said, would place a tremendous strain on the finances of the company. Probably all the reserves would be needed in addition to heavy borrowing. The increase in hiring, especially of expensive experts, would hurt the morale of Jet Power's employees. In general, all these considerations would be harmful to the company. Production, sales, and profit would all be affected seriously. It was Jenning's recommendation that the company forget about Saturn X and instead produce new variations on the products that had already gained market acceptance or find new markets for the old products.

Winthrop suggested that an early, unsolicited proposal to NASA might be a way to sound them out on their acceptance of Saturn X without going through expensive changes in the company. Jennings replied that this might be an acceptable alternative, except that, in order to be credible, the proposal would need to be supported by many of the changes needed if the company were actually to produce such an engine. It would be necessary to, at the least, perform research and development to the point where a feasible innovation in such engines could be described. This would mean considerable beefing up of the engineering department, plus investment in new facilities and equipment.

Obviously, the only saving would be in production and delivery facilities which could be acquired only in the event a contract was won. In any case, there would have to be a sizeable investment with high risk because of a low probability market potential. The risk would not only be for the R&D investment, but also for the present standing of the company. Many of its best engineering people might be lost and, if Saturn X failed and layoffs began, the company's attractiveness to new employees, would be lost. It might become difficult to maintain Jet Power's leadership.

Even the current fully developed products required some engineering know-how in order to maintain quality. If older engineers should leave because of the Saturn X project, they would take that know-how with them. This would damage marketing by the company.

Despite these warning's, Winthrop still felt that a very large profit potential existed for the Saturn X engine. He believed that the risk might not appear as great, if a careful analysis were made. He requested that Jennings prepare a plan for the project and also research the market, not only for the large engine, but also for any new products. He presented his own evaluation of the situation as follows:

1. In the next 5 years, the market for current products will have reached a plateau caused by increased competition, reduced public interest in the space program, and reduced government expenditures in this field. He estimated that the profit at that time would be, with no change in the company's policies and plans, $8 million with a probability of 0.70. The expectation for this plan was $5.6 million.
2. For the same period, Jet Power could find a new market in space programs by strapping together two or more of their larger engines to make a more powerful package. Also, they could develop a new jet engine for the supersonic transport airplane that was being pushed by the Federal Government. Under this plan, the estimated return was $15 million with a probability of 0.15 with an expectation of $2.25 million.
3. By pursuing the Saturn X project, Winthrop believed that 5 years would be sufficient time to reach a return of $50 million and a .15 probability. The expectation would then be $7.5 million.

It was quite evident that Winthrop had little faith in the second plan as a solution to the problem of reduced earnings for Jet Power and felt that Saturn X was the only satisfactory solution despite its low probability of success.

As was expected, Jennings' study verified that the market for huge booster engines was already overcrowded with well established competitors and that the potential was very low, particularly because of escalation of the war in Vietnam. Congress, in reviewing the budget, had made large slashes in the manned space programs and had gone on record opposing further expansions in that area. If the company decided in favor of Saturn X, it would need to invest $10 million dollars in research and new facilities. Further, for the moment, there were no engineers with the necessary experience available at any price. Therefore, Jennings gave Saturn X a probability of success of 0.05. Winthrop, while conceding that Jennings was not mistaken in his overall analysis, felt that he could always persuade (with a generous financial arrangement) one of the experts now with one of the other large firms to join Jet Power. In addition, one of his contacts in NASA had assured him that their setback in Congress was only temporary and that there would be a tremendous increase in the manned space program in an attempt to catch up with the Russian efforts. Winthrop agreed that his probability estimate should be modified, and he compromised on 0.10.

On the second plan, Jennings saw a much smaller capital risk. An

TABLE 7.1   JET POWER INC. PLANNING CHART

Plan	Revised Probability	Estimated Return ($MM)	Expectation
One	.65	8	5.2
Two	.25	15	3.75
Three	.10	50	5.0

investment of only $2 million in research, sales, and new facilities might be adequate. There would be no upheaval of personnel and, in fact, there would be an improvement in the morale due to the introduction of new products. Jennings thought the probability of success should be 0.25. Winthrop had no facts which could affect this estimate. This left a probability of 0.65 for the first plan.

The revised expectations are shown in Table 7.1.

The average expectation was $4.65 million. The deviations from the average for each plan were as follows:

Plan	Deviation
One	+0.55
Two	−0.90
Three	+0.35

Plan Two appeared to be a poor choice but it was difficult to decide between the others. Further examination of the figures and the addition of weightings based on the financial risk involved proved Plan One to be the best choice. In addition, Saturn X had a large disadvantage in that the entire future of the company would be at stake on a single, low probability of success scheme.

Science had only succeeded in proving to Winthrop that Saturn X would be an unwise choice. At this point, Winthrop had to exercise some of the superior judgment for which he was being paid. He knew that no business could thrive without some risk and that the larger risks usually went with the greater opportunities. He was convinced of a rosy future for space programs and equally convinced that a conservative approach would not give Jet Power the share of the market it desired. He, therefore, without hesitation, picked Plan Two.

We know now that the space programs have since wound down and that the supersonic airplane is a dead issue. We cannot fault Winthrop, because he was looking ahead only 5 years from 1969. His decision was probably a good one. But we can apply DCR principles to this planning problem and see whether we would arrive at the same decision.

Assuming a constant 5% growth rate, the company's net worth in 1974 would be $510 million if no new liabilities were assumed. Therefore, Plan One (status quo) would have a profitability index in 1974 of 0.015.

Plan Two (strapping engines together) would require $2 million additional investment. Since the company had only small cash reserves, this money would need to be borrowed. The net worth would then be reduced by $3 million (liability and cost of borrowing). The 1974 profitability index for Plan Two would be 0.029.

Finally, the net worth for Plan Three, Saturn X, would be $496.5 million and the profitability index, 0.10. The exceptionally high PI makes the Saturn X project very tempting, but the reasons for Winthrop's rejection of this venture were too sound to be ignored. We too must reject it. Plan Two with a PI about twice as large as Plan One was an obvious choice. Note that probabilities and uncertainties still entered into this decision in the estimates of sales volume but to a lesser degree. If there was a 50% error in the profit estimate of Plan Two, the PI would drop to 0.014 which was still comparable to that of Plan One, even if the Plan One profit estimate were exactly right. But a much higher profit was possible with Plan Two, and so the risk was not very high.

Another consideration was that the PI of Plan One indicated that this business was decreasing, and Jet Power had to consider a new plan of action to save its profitability.

MAINTAINING THE PROGRAM

The best of organizations may do a fine job of planning and still fail to achieve any of the objectives of the plan. Dynamic cost reduction becomes static, if there is no provision for auditing the operations, making needed corrections, and ensuring the continuation of the program beyond the initial changes. The existing management information system need not be altered to provide the necessary data for monitoring the DCR program. The program does not require unique data or reporting charts.

An important factor is motivating department heads to become involved in implementing a DCR program and to remain interested in its perpetuation. DCR has in its favor that drastic measures like layoffs are rarely needed. Cost reduction programs usually mean an influx of

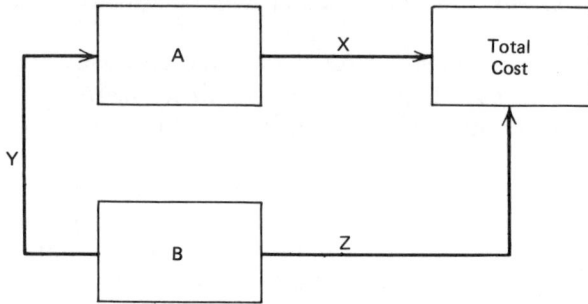

Total Cost = X + Z

Figure 36   DCR Control Network

"outsiders" wielding their axes and scissors with little respect for anybody or anything. DCR, except in terminal cases, is a much gentler activity and so is far better received.

In addition, departmental heads are members of the planning committee and, therefore, help to develop the new cost standards. The changes that may be needed in the respective departments are determined by the heads of these departments and not by some unfeeling outsider.

Since the DCR program is their program, the department heads will more readily accept new reporting systems to monitor the program and control it. Actually, only one new device is needed. *Existing reporting systems will not need to be disturbed except to add any necessary items not presently supplied.* The new technique is a combination of sensitivity analysis and PERT (see Chapter 6 for an explanation of PERT). The DCR control network uses the PERT format but deals only in dollar costs and not with time schedules. Also, it is not probabilistic. Figure 36 is a typical DCR control network.

The only purpose of the network is to establish the relationship between the various costs. The cost accounting system can supply the same information, but the network is more readily read when the interrelationships are complex and there are many items. In Figure 36, A and B are processes or operations such as cutting, drilling, or plating. X is the cost contribution to the total for process A. Z is B's contribution to the total for process A. Z is B's contribution to the total cost and Y is that part of X which comes from B. The total cost is X + Z. X is actually the sum of Y and some A cost.

Reporting on this particular network is shown in Table 7.2.

Note that both X and Y are out of tolerance. However, X is out only

TABLE 7.2 DCR PROGRAM REPORTING CHART

Cost	Standard	Tolerance	Actual ($) Wk. Endg. 6/7	6/14
X	2.0	0.1	2.0	2.2
Y	1.0	0.05	1.0	1.15
Z	5.0	0.2	5.2	5.2

0.1 and Y is up exactly 0.1. From the network, we know that X's excess of 0.1 is due to Y. Therefore, correction need be made only to Y.

In some cases, it may be more convenient to display X, Y, and Z in terms of labor hours. They would then need translation into dollars for management reporting. Using labor hours, at least for factory operations, permits the retention of existing reporting charts.

Motivation is the secret of success for any management activity. Involving all department heads in the control process is an excellent way of providing the motivation. To ensure the continuation of the DCR program, a review meeting should be held at regular intervals, say monthly. At each meeting, all managers will be able to see the jigsaw of DCR control network put together and learn how well their efforts have succeeded. At the review meeting, new inputs can be plugged in and adjustments made to cost standards as required. If top management is concerned enough to make these meetings motivating and rewarding, enthusiasm for the program will continue.

Many very large organizations have cost improvement programs that depend on employee suggestions. The employees are given money rewards. On paper, the savings are monstrously high, but the improvements are, in most cases, just that, paper savings. That's because the suggestions affect isolated items rarely touching on the really expensive areas. With DCR, savings are in the sensitive areas. The rewards to management, in profitability, are much greater than with conventional cost improvement programs. It appears reasonable that some financial rewards be offered those involved in implementing the DCR program. A job well done is not always enough satisfaction, even for the most idealistic of managers.

All cost reduction programs cost something. DCR programs cost less than most and have the greatest impact on profit. It would seem reasonable to offer bonuses or other rewards for maintaining high levels of profitability. Perhaps the improvement in a profit sharing plan is sufficient reward.

SUMMARY

An effective DCR program must not be a temporary measure, else the improvements will vanish with time. Where productivity accepts the limitations of a specific situation, profitability demands rejection of the situation and adoption of a new organization.

The purposes of the individuals in a company are not necessarily the same as the company purpose. DCR demands that all be integrated into a single purpose—profitability. The preferred DCR organization is a team effort for planning and goal setting to shorten the communication link. For large companies, this may mean splitting into a number of independent profit centers. Each profit center would have its own supports, such as marketing, production, or engineering. Each would have its own planning committee.

There is a strong temptation to rely heavily on outside consultants for most cost reduction programs. There is a need for consultants to assist in the formative stage of the DCR program. Thereafter, consultant skills required are sharply defined by the program so that such skills can be purchased by specification and with competitive bidding.

Planning steps follow:

1. Gathering information on the environment. Market research should be in depth.
2. Gathering information on the internal environment.
3. Identify and study the factors which may limit the organization's profitability and growth in the future.
4. Establish the objectives or goals of the business.
5. Analyze all alternatives.
6. Select best alternatives.
7. Determine actions needed to achieve objectives.
8. Develop time schedule for the actions.
9. Prepare master plan.

An important factor in maintaining the DCR program is motivation. DCR has an edge in this area because of participation in the planning by all managers affected by the program. A second advantage is in the improvement in profit-sharing programs because of DCR. Existing reporting systems need not be abandoned. They are supplemented by new cost accounting reports and a special PERT-like control network. The only purpose of the network is to establish the relationship between the various costs.

REFERENCES

1. J. M. Pfiffner and F. P. Sherwood, *"Administrative Organization,"* Prentice-Hall, Englewood Cliffs, New Jersey, 1960, p. 30.
2. R. A. Johnson, et. al., *"The Theory and Management of Systems,"* McGraw-Hill, New York, 1963, Chapter 3.
3. M. Haire, *"Modern Organization Theory,"* John Wiley and Sons, New York, 1959, p. 50.
4. R. Carzo and J. N. Yanouzas, "Effects of Flat and Tall Organization Structure," *Administrative Science Quarterly*, vol. 14, no. 2, pp. 178–191, June 1969.
5. S. Thompson, "How Companies Plan," *American Management Association*, Research Study No. 54, New York, 1962.

CHAPTER 8

DCR CASE STUDIES

To demonstrate the power of the DCR tool we shall consider several special applications in this chapter. In one case, we shall learn why a start up failed to obtain financing. Another will be a demonstration of DCR principles used to evaluate an investment. The third case concerns a non-profit hospital and how DCR could be applied to its problem.

IDL INDUSTRIES

The information that follows is taken from an actual 1974 business plan.

IDL Industries (IDLI) plans to specialize in the sales and service of electronics for hotels and motels. Its primary product is a room television system in which the conventional master antenna system is replaced with a video distribution system. Advantages of the system are: 30% less energy consumption by receivers, many closed-circuit channels available for special guest services, better quality picture and sound, and remote channel selection in every room. This system is economically feasible for new construction. For existing systems, IDLI offers customized room receivers, free upgrading of distribution system, low cost servicing, and inexpensive hotel-owned pay-TV systems (no black boxes in rooms). An unrelated secondary product is an invention of a marine navigation system that will be developed as a joint venture by IDLI and the XXXX Corp. Both products have extremely high potential.

IDLI proposes to capture a minute portion of the total U.S. color TV receiver market. The current total market is about 8 million receivers. About 450,000 color sets are sold to hotels/motels, about 5% of the total market. The IDLI 5-year goal is 10% of the hotel market or about one-half of 1% of the total market. This represents only about 50,000 units but equates to about $6 million in annual sales at an estimated profit of 15–20% before taxes.

The IDLI goal for the navigation invention is a $500 unit for sale to pleasure craft. Boating is a $3 billion industry. IDLI estimates that annual sales for the navigation equipment should be about $1 million. Development of the invention would be through government funded study programs at the XXXX Corp. laboratories. The latter company would concentrate on the military and industrial markets leaving the pleasure markets to IDLI.

IDLI requires about $30,000 initially to be used exclusively for marketing expenses (advertising, presentations, demonstration showroom, etc.). No salaries would be drawn by management until the viability of the company is proven by sales. An initial tentative order for 2500 receivers has been received from a retirement village. Startup would require about $100,000 for interim financing of the retirement village deal and another $100,000 for operating capital. It is expected that all additional funds needed will be obtained by means of short term inventory loans and/or factoring.

The preceding is essentially the summary that appeared in the front of the business plan which was presented to a firm of venture capitalists. The plan was immediately rejected for several reasons.

Venture capital firms, when investing in technical companies, look for high technology, preferably a breakthrough in the state-of-the-art. The summary did not indicate such a breakthrough.

Venture capital investors want either a substantial quick profit in a short time (sometimes as little as one year) or a very large profit (perhaps ten times their investment) over a longer period. The summary gave no hint of either possibility. The relatively small capitalization requested ($230,000) and the projected annual sales of $6 million were all the clues the investors needed.

It is not suggested that a DCR approach to preparation of the business plan would have changed the minds of the financiers. We do suggest that the DCR approach might have alerted IDLI to the weaknesses of the plan. With corrections, investors might be found with objectives different from those of venture capitalists. There are many investors who would be glad to finance a company that promises stability and reasonable growth.

Market Research

IDLI did excellent market research to support their estimates of potential sales. Based on data from the U.S. Department of Commerce,

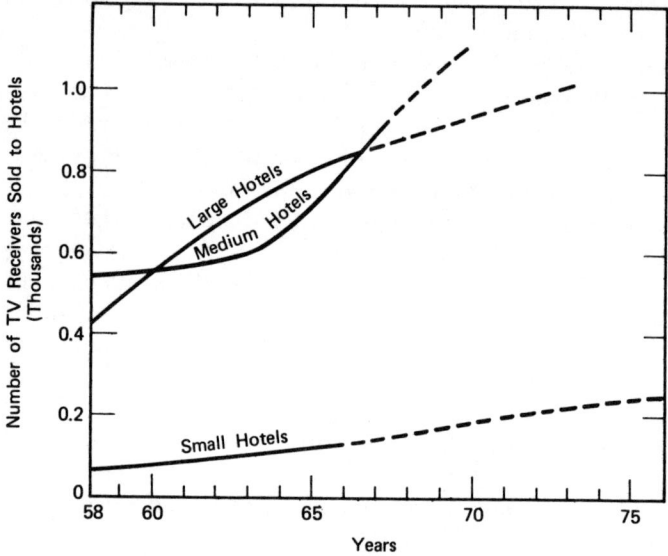

Figure 37   TV Receivers Sold to Hotels

Moody's Industrial Manual, and other sources, they plotted the curves of Figure 37 and 38.

Zenith was the leader of the competition with 20% of the market. IDLI felt that this was true for the hotel/motel market as well. Motorola was third with 10%. Also, the hotel/motel market was only

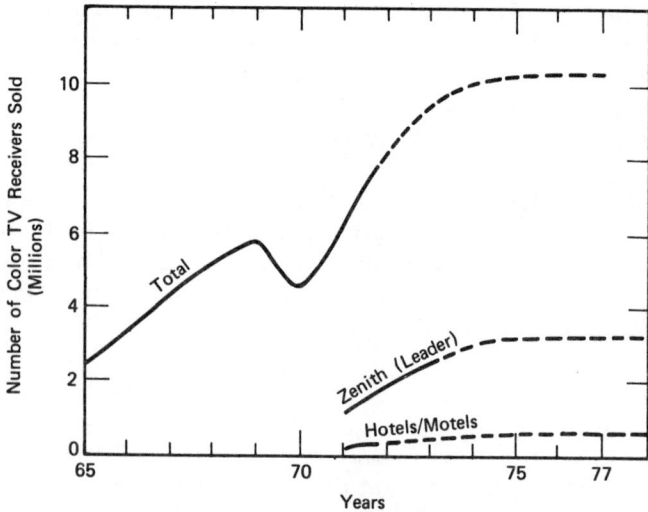

Figure 38   Color TV Market

TABLE 8.1 HOTEL TV RECEIVER COMPETITION

	Large Hotels			Medium Hotels			Small Hotels		
	Zenith	Philco	IDLI	Zenith	Philco	IDLI	Zenith	Philco	IDLI
Custom Design	No	No	Yes	No	No	Yes	No	No	No
Remote Control	No	No	Yes	No	No	Yes	No	No	No
19-inch Color	Yes	Yes	Yes	Yes	Yes	Yes	Yes	Yes	Yes
CCTV Feature	No	No	Yes	No	No	Yes	No	No	No
Wakeup Service	No	No	Yes	No	No	Yes	No	No	Yes
Years Warranty	1	2	5	1	2	5	1	2	5
Price ($)	300	320	350	320	340	350	340	360	340
5 Yrs. Service ($)	200	150	0	200	150	0	200	150	0
Total	500	470	350	520	490	350	540	510	340
Replacement ($)	600	564	400	624	588	400	648	612	390
5 Yr. Lease ($)	675	720	500	720	765	500	765	810	500
Lease Renewal ($)	810	864	500	864	918	600	918	972	600

5% of the total market and the hotel/motel market was growing at a lower rate than the total market. For that reason, IDLI did not anticipate any strong effort by the giants to capture larger shares of the hotel/motel market. Table 8.1 was developed to determine IDLI's ability to compete in the three hotel markets against the possible marketing strategies.

The plan further noted that if the profit was large enough, it was conceivable that the competition could cut prices. According to the 1973 Moody's Industrial Manual:

	Percent Profit	
	1971	*1972*
Zenith	10	8
Motorola	7	8

Since these are two of the leaders, it is safe to assume that those with smaller market shares do not have larger profit margins. In order to compete effectively with IDLI, the manufacturers of conventional receivers would need to sell below cost with little hope (in such a highly competitive market) of improving their share of the total market by more than a minute amount.

Based on a preliminary sales campaign which turned up tentative sales of about 2000 rooms in Las Vegas, Nevada, IDLI estimated its projected market share as follows:

	Year				
	1	*2*	*3*	*4*	*5*
Estimated total Market ($MM)	225	250	275	300	325
IDLI Share (%)	1.0	1.6	2.5	4.0	6.1
IDLI Sales ($MM)	3	4	7	12	20

The $20 million sales would have interested the venture capitalists in light of the small investment required. It was unfortunate that this did not appear in the summary.

Financial Plan

We next examine the profit and loss forecast and the pro forma balance sheet which appeared in the plan. The significant financial data is shown in Table 8.2.

TABLE 8.2 IDLI FINANCIAL DATA

	Year		
	1	2	3
Sales	0	$3,009,000	$13,045,000
Operating Expenses	$ 171,470	1,723,200	3,623,300
Cost of Sales	17,600	22,480	23,830
G&A	72,970	166,325	241,525
Total Costs	268,577	1,990,065	4,108,155
Gross	(268,577)	1,018,935	8,936,845
Tax	0	259,449	4,467,771
Net	(268,577)	758,486	4,468,074
Percent	—	38	108
Assets	1,126,248	4,660,134	7,364,136
Liabilities	589,210	1,998,649	6,667,777
Net Worth	$ 537,038	$2,661,485	$ 696,359
PI	—	0.28	6.0

The profits grow to an amazing 108% in the third year. This is reflected in the PI value, 6.0. Obviously this is not very likely for a new firm in a very competitive industry. The plan, in describing weaknesses, confessed to a lack of skills in financial management. If an accountant had been a member of the management team, he would never have permitted the plan to be submitted. It is no wonder that investors were not interested.

A closer examination uncovered the reason for the unbelievable financial data. IDLI had planned to rely on short term bank loans and factoring for operating capital. This is not a viable method for a new company to employ. A more reasonable scheme, and one more acceptable to investors, would have been to ask for capital investments large enough to carry the company through two years of no or little profit. Also, it is incredible that hotels/motels would pay cash for the systems. One must expect reduced revenue, because of discounts on accounts receivable paper and uncollectables. In any case, a new company cannot expect a sizable cash flow in its early years. The cash flow shown in this business plan is totally unbelievable.

Table 8.3 is adjusted financial data that would have repaired this business plan. Of course, there is no guarantee that venture capitalists would be interested. To gain their interest, IDLI should have presented data on the navigation invention. The fact that a major company

TABLE 8.3   REVISED FINANCIAL DATA

	1	2	3
		Year	
Sales	0	$1,500,000	$6,000,000
Costs	$ 268,577	1,990,065	4,108,155
Gross	(268,577)	(490,065)	1,891,845
Tax	0	0	566,602
Net	(268,577)	(490,065)	1,325,243
Percent	—	—	32
Assets	1,126,248	3,795,377	7,364,136
Liabilities	686,827	1,559,449	5,113,208
Net Worth	$ 439,421	$2,235,928	$2,250,928
PI	—	—	0.58

was involved in a joint venture with IDLI to develop it could have attracted many investors.

This table is based on the more conservative sales forecast that appeared earlier in the plan. The 32% profit is still too high but can be explained by the fact that the receivers are sold directly to the consumer so that all profits go to IDLI and none to middlemen.

The plan is still not attractive to investors, particularly because of the lack of growth potential. The net worth has not increased despite the large profit rate. To attract investors it is necessary to expand on the navigation invention. The big plus in that area is that a well known, large company has agreed to a joint venture in the development of the navigation equipment. The television receiver business could then be presented as the bread and butter line supporting the entry into the boating industry. The potential for growth would be very attractive to would-be investors.

One must conclude that the venture capitalists were quite correct in their rejection of the plan. Their reason was probably a lack of enthusiasm for a new entry into a highly competitive industry. Our reason is a lack of potential for growth. We are sure that the men who formed IDLI were mislead by the estimates of sales volume into believing that theirs would be a growth company.

THE MASON FUND

The Mason Fund is a closed-end, nondiversified investment company. The primary investment objective is long term capital appreciation, with a secondary objective of preservation of capital and current income. Most investors judge such funds by the price-equity (P/E) ratio. The price is the current price of the shares on the market. Equity is that share of the company's assets allocated to a single share.

The Mason Fund had 10 million shares outstanding. The current assets were $40,181,103 making the equity per share, $4.02. The latest price quoted for the shares is $24.375, making the P/E, 6.0. The Mason Fund was "good" investment.

Unfortunately this is a poor way to evaluate the Fund. It is necessary to examine the Fund's financial reports. The current report supplies the following data:

Assets	$40,181,103
Liabilities	488,190
	$40,669,293
Income	$664,268
Expenses	103,943
Gross	$560,325
Taxes	50,000
Net	$510,325

The profitability index is computed to be 0.012. This is an extremely low figure indicating that the money invested is not earning enough. The reason lies in the objectives of the Fund—long term capital appreciation and preservation of the capital. All the income stems from interest and dividends received while the Fund is holding securities. This income can not ever be large and is not important to the Fund's objectives or to the investors. What is important is the capital gains derived from security transactions. Some understanding of this is obtained from the Fund's financial report.

Net realized gain on sales of investments		$5,131,496
Net unrealized appreciation		1,918,366
Increase in net assets		$7,049,862
Net assets at end	$40,181,103	
Net assets at start	33,131,241	
Net increase	$ 7,049,862	

This means a 21% capital gain. On the face of it, one might conclude that the Fund is performing well. But one must realize that the gain represents a paper profit caused by a rise in the stock market. The gain has little or no bearing on the profitability of the companies whose securities are being bought and sold. The gain is only realizable if the securities are sold at a price higher than their purchase price. Even then, most of the increase in assets will only be reinvested or used to compensate for losses on other investments. That is because the investors in the Fund hope to make a substantial profit by the sale of their Fund shares when the price has gone high enough.

Comparing the Fund's one year growth with New York Stock Exchange companies with the same P/E:

	Percent
Mason Fund	21
Natl. Medical Enterp.	19
Intl. Multifoods	17

The Fund is not doing much better than the market. In fact, it is doing worse than many of the better performers. For example:

Sea Cont. Unit.	37%
Schlumberger Ltd.	23
Sambo's Rest.	25

The obvious conclusion is that the Mason Fund is not a good investment. It is not even good for speculation. Either is better found among the securities of many companies listed on the exchanges. And such securities have the advantage of being more readily evaluated with the DCR technique.

THE WILSON FOUNDATION AND HOSPITAL

The Wilson Foundation and Hospital are related nonprofit corporations. The Foundation receives, holds, and manages all funds contributed to it primarily for the support of the Hospital. Several independent fund raising groups frequently assist the Hospital, while other outside entities have endowment-type funds held in trust for distribution to the Hospital.

The Hospital, like many others, faced some difficult problems. The spiralling cost of professional liability insurance is one of them. Another financial burden results from increasing government involvement in the provision of health care and growing government regulations, coupled with Medicare payments at a rate less than the actual cost of the care.

Inflation has affected all goods and services required by the Hospital. The Hospital must add highly trained professional staff and modern equipment. This translates into increased operating costs.

The Hospital balance sheet is much more complex than that of industry. For example, there is deferred revenue from government sponsored contractual programs. Total revenue for these monies are included in patient service revenue. However, the government does reduce such revenues to the extent it exceeds estimated reimbursable costs. As a result, the Hospital needs to list as a liability the amount of this reduction.

Other unusual items are specific purpose funds (pledges and bequests) and restricted funds (used only for specific purposes such as research). For the purpose of the balance sheet, such institutions show fund balances instead of shareholders equity. Tables 8.4 and 8.5 provide the financial data for the Hospital for the years 1975 and 1976.

The balance sheet shows a 10.4% increase in net worth. Since investments and patient receivables can account for only a small part of this and accounts payable have risen 15.6%, the net worth increase can

TABLE 8.4   WILSON FUND AND HOSPITAL BALANCE SHEET

	1976	1975
Assets		
Cash	$ 379,000	$ 252,000
Patient receivables	3,202,000	3,089,000
Bequest receivables	1,217,000	710,000
Inventories	356,000	442,000
Prepaid expenses	94,000	59,000
Due restricted funds	452,000	—
Security investments	3,855,000	3,393,000
Real estate investments	804,000	595,000
Plant and equipment	11,420,000	11,021,000
Specific purpose funds	12,260,000	10,819,000
Endowment funds	1,738,000	1,640,000
Total assets	$35,777,000	$32,020,000
Liabilities		
Accounts payable	$2,094,000	$ 1,811,000
Accrued cost reimbursement	175,000	240,000
Insurance advances	63,000	65,000
Deferred insurance revenue	237,000	222,000
Due from restricted funds	452,000	—
Total liabilities	$ 3,021,000	$ 2,338,000
Net worth	$32,756,000	$29,682,000

TABLE 8.5   WILSON FUND AND HOSPITAL REVENUE STATEMENT

	1976	1975
Revenue		
Patient service	$14,418,000	$12,642,000
Other	770,000	703,000
Gifts and bequests	3,540,000	2,745,000
Investment income	378,000	319,000
Investment sales gain	182,000	22.000
Total revenue	$19,288,000	$16,431,000
Expenses		
Patient service	$ 2,255,000	$ 1,469,000
Operations	15,250,000	13,776,000
Non-operating	513,000	451,000
Total expenses	$18,018,000	$15,696,000
Excess	$ 1,270,000	$ 735,000

only be attributed to a rise in bequests. Note that bequest receivables increased 71.4%.

From Table 8.5, we find that revenue in excess of operating expenses increased 72.7%, approximately the same amount as the increase in bequests. Calculating profitability indices and using the excess revenue as the profit, we find 0.025 for 1975 and 0.039 for 1976. This represents a 56.7% increase.

A serious problem now faced the Board of Directors. In both years, operating expenses exceeded operating revenue. In 1975, the "loss" was $1,900,000 and in 1976, $2,317,000. The loss had increased 22%. The Hospital had been fortunate that gifts and bequests had more than compensated for the deficit. Note that only unrestricted funds could be used for this purpose. The changes from 1975 to 1976 were as follows:

Patient revenue	+8.9%
Operating expense	+10.7%
Gifts	+28.9%
Non-operating expense	+13.7%

The Board needed to ensure meeting future operating budgets and, at the same time, were anxious to construct a new research laboratory for cancer research. They needed to plan for at least the next 5 years. This meant considering all the factors affecting the expenses and the revenue.

Patient revenue would reflect some of the inflation-related costs. This would be reduced to a large degree by the lag in Medicare reimbursement levels. The government is rather slow in making suitable adjustments. There was some noise in Washington about national health insurance, but it was very unlikely that this would come in time to help the Wilson Hospital. The Board assumed that the inflation rate would average about 8% a year for patient revenue. The free and part-pay allowance would be as high as 12% in 5 years. The Board estimated that patient service revenue in 1981 would be 40% greater than that of 1976 or $20,185,000. This would be reduced by 12% (part-pay allowance) to become $17,763,000.

Operating expenses would have the same increase due to inflation of 40%, plus a 20% increase in professional service salaries. Malpractice insurance rates were expected to stabilize within the next year. The estimate of operating expenses for 1981 thus became:

Professional services	$13,792,000
Other expenses	9,282,000
Total operating expenses	$23,074,000
Revenue	17,763,000
1981 operating deficit	$ 5,311,000

This, of course, needs to be modified by the non-operating surplus or deficit. Usually, this would be a surplus, because it is chiefly made up of unrestricted gifts and bequests. Such revenue increased 28% in 1976 over 1975 gifts, but such increases can not be expected every year despite inflation. There is tremendous competition for donations by too many worthy causes. Then, too, there are limitations on tax deductions for charitable contributions. A reasonable increase by 1981 would be 40%. Assuming nonoperating expenses would equal approximately the income and gain from investments, the nonoperating revenue should be $4,956,000. Then the net excess revenue would be $355,000 (difference between operating deficit and non-operating revenue).

This is bad news, because we are dealing with estimates. These estimates could be as much as $500,000 in error, resulting in a deficit in the use of unrestricted funds. We still have the problem of adding costs for the research laboratory.

The problem can be approached in another manner. Note that the net worth increased 10% in one year. Assume it will do the same for the next 5 years. Then the net worth in 1981 will be $49,134,000. A PI of about 0.03 appears to be a *desirable goal,* based on 1976 and 1975

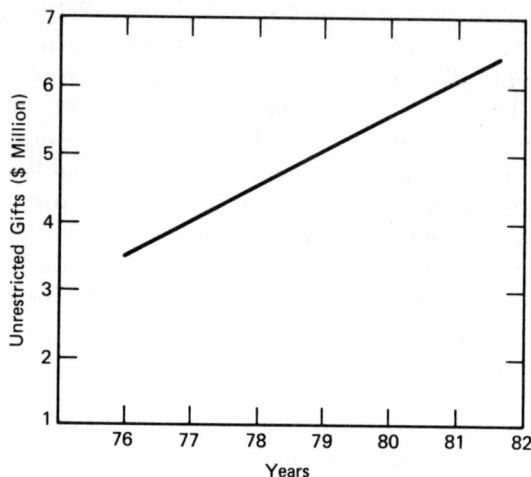

Figure 39   Goals for Unrestricted Gifts

balance sheets. A PI of 0.03 and a net worth of $49,134,000 gives as a *goal excess revenue* $1,474,000. The difference between this value and the previously computed $355,000 is $1,119,000. The *goal for unrestricted gifts* is increased by that amount to $6,075,000. This goal can be used to calculate the goals for each year between 1976 and 1981. This is done by plotting the actual for 1976 and the goal for 1981 and drawing a straight line between the two points as in Figure 39.

From the chart, the goal for contributions is $4 million for 1977, $4.5 million for 1978, and so forth. These are goals to ensure that there will be no deficit and no need to draw on invested funds. If the goals are exceeded, the surplus are available to bolster poor years. Underachievement of goals is a warning that other sources of funds must be found. Each year the data should be recalculated. This will serve to make each succeeding goal more accurate.

It is evident that the research laboratory can not be funded from unrestricted gifts. The Board of Directors must, therefore, look to sources of restricted funds and grants for this improvement.

Exercises for the Reader

What has gone before has served to introduce the profitability concept and DCR. The case studies that follow will give the reader an opportunity to practice applying DCR principles to an actual problem. There is no single correct solution to either case. The best solution is

the one that offers the greatest improvement over a productivity concept approach. This is illustrated in the Peabody Company case, in
which the chief protagonists are both committed to productivity. For
the Whistle Toy Company, one should develop both productivity and
profitability plans for comparison.

THE PEABODY COMPANY

The Peabody Company is a medium sized manufacturer of automobile
parts. It has two plants, one producing three kinds of automatic trans-
mission valves and the other, three different accessories.

The sales manager, Nicholas Di Falco, was a science oriented type,
who very carefully planned his operations. To achieve a maximum in
his department, he determined the absolute and relative market potentials, based chiefly on his salesmen's estimates. He set up territorial
objectives derived from the market potentials and salesmen's reports
on customers, and prepared a plan for achieving these objectives. For
the year 1971, Di Falco collected information that permitted him to
assign a relative rating to each sales territory normally covered
throughout the continental United States. He plotted the curve in
Figure 40 to show the relationship between the territory rating and the
percent of United States sales potential for each product of the company. The rating is actually a multiplier of the potential sales to give
the estimated sales volume. Thus, for Product A a territory with a

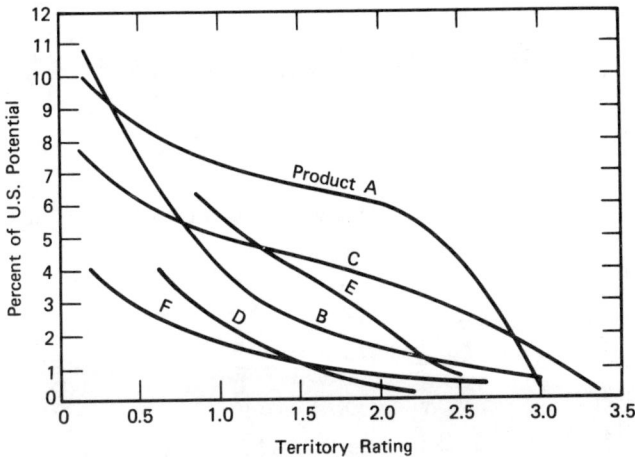

Figure 40   Percent Potential versus Territory Rating

TABLE 8.6 ESTIMATED SALES VS NUMBER OF SALESMEN

178

Territory	Prod.	1970 Sales ($000)	1970 Sales Per Man ($000)	Rating From Curve	1971 Estimated Sales/Man ($000)	1971 Total Sales ($000)	Cost Of Sales ($000)	1971 Net ($000)
4%, 25 men	A	2000	80	2.68	214	5360		
	B	500	20	1.05	21	525		
	C	1000	40	1.9	76	1900		
	D	650	26	0.65	17	423		
	E	1500	60	1.5	90	2250		
	F	250	10	0.22	2	55		
Total						10,513	625	9,888
3%, 33 men	A	2000	60	2.75	165	5445		
	B	500	15	1.3	20	660		
	C	1000	30	2.5	75	2475		
	D	650	19	0.85	16	528		
	E	1500	45	1.85	83	2739		
	F	250	8	0.45	4	132		
Total						11,979	825	11,154
2%, 50 men	A	2000	40	2.85	114	5700		
	B	500	10	1.8	18	900		
	C	1000	20	2.85	57	2850		
	D	650	13	1.2	16	800		
	E	1500	30	2.15	65	3250		
	F	250	5	0.95	5	250		
Total						13,750	1250	12,500
1%, 100 men	A	2000	20	2.95	59	5900		
	B	500	5	2.7	14	1400		
	C	1000	10	3.2	32	3200		
	D	650	7	1.65	12	1200		
	E	1500	15	2.55	38	3800		
	F	250	3	1.8	5	500		
Total						16,000	2500	13,500

potential of 4% has the rating (from the curve) of 2.68. Total sales in 1970 for Product A was $2,000,000 for that territory.

Di Falco would like to know the optimum number of salesmen to use. Optimum is that number which would result in the maximum net profit. The philosophy that Di Falco has developed from his experience is that a high potential territory needs less salesmen than one with a low potential. Therefore, he expects that the number of salesmen will be inversely proportional to the potential of a territory. Di Falco suspected that there would be a maximum number of salesmen that could be placed in a territory beyond which the profit would not be increased sufficiently to pay for the selling costs.

In order to determine the best number of salesmen to employ, Di Falco calculated the net for a range from 25 salesmen in a 4% territory to 100 in a 1% territory. He listed the figures in Table 8.6.

Di Falco's calculations were made in the following manner:

$$\text{1970 Sales per man} = \frac{\text{1970 total sales}}{\text{Number of salesmen}}$$

$$\text{For Product A and 25 men, 1970 sales per man} = \frac{2,000,000}{25}$$
$$= \$80,000$$

$$\text{Estimated 1971 sales per man} = 2.68 \times 80,000 = \$214,400$$

$$\text{Assumed cost per salesman (salary, bonus, travel, and supervision)} = \$25,000$$

$$\text{Net for Product A in the territory} = \text{Total 1971 sales}$$
$$\text{minus cost of sales} = 25 \times 214,400 - 25 \times 25,000$$
$$= \$4,735,000$$

The demand for automobile parts and accessories come from population centers so that a territory that buys 4% of the output of Product A will generally buy 4% of the output of the other products. Therefore, all the 4% outputs of all the products are assumed to be in the same territory.

The curve in Figure 41 was plotted using the values from Table 8.6. A sharp rise is noted between 25 and 40 men on the curve, which then flattens out. A twofold increase in the number of salesmen from 50 to 100 does not produce as much added income as the increase from 25 to 50. This told Di Falco that about 50 men was an optimum number for his sales force.

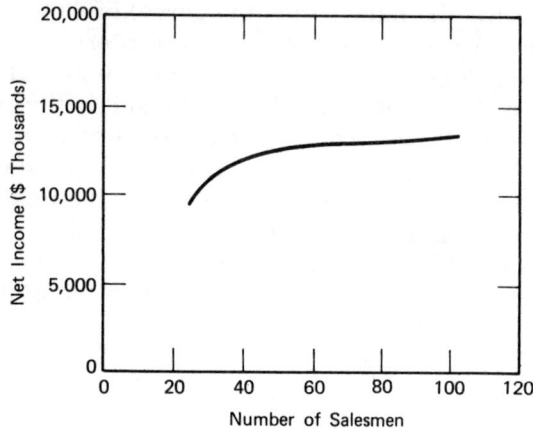

Figure 41   Number of Salesmen versus Income

When this analysis was presented to management, a loud protest came from the vice president of manufacturing. He, John Tolliver, objected on two counts. First, Di Falco had failed to consider the costs of producing the items in computing the income. Second, the sales department should push the products that contributed the most profit, not the ones that were easiest to sell. The increased volume of the low profit products might not be sufficient to equal the return that could be realized from a small increment in the sales of high profit items. Tolliver felt that these considerations might make a large difference in the manning of the sales staff. He presented the following figures to support his arguments:

    Plant One (Products A, B, C)
              Total Fixed Costs $938,200
    Plant Two (Products D, E, F)
              Total Fixed Costs $357,600

Variable costs for each product are shown in Figure 42.

Tolliver then made new tabulations of Di Falco's data with the addition of the production costs resulting in Table 8.7.

Again, a curve is plotted (Figure 43) to show the relation between the number of salesmen and the net income. This time there is a sharp knee in the curve at approximately 33 salesmen. This was a clear cut indication that the optimum choice was that number, as Tolliver saw it. On the other hand, Di Falco pointed out that the curve began to rise again, reaching a peak at 100 men. He saw it as a decision to be made

TABLE 8.7 REVISED ESTIMATED SALES

Territory	Product	1971 Est. Sales ($000)	Variable Costs ($000)	Net ($000)	Plant One + Plant Two Fixed Costs ($000)	Cost Of Sales ($000)	1971 Net Return ($000)
4%, 25 men	A	5360	2350	3010			
	B	525	220	305			
	C	1900	700	1200			
	D	423	105	318			
	E	2250	690	1560			
	F	55	—	55			
Total		6448		7559	1296	625	4527
3%, 33 men	A	5445	2350	3095			
	B	660	300	330			
	C	2475	880	1595			
	D	528	110	418			
	E	2739	750	1989			
	F	132	—	132			
Total				7559	1296	825	5438
2%, 50 men	A	5700	2390	2610			
	B	900	380	520			
	C	2850	980	1870			
	D	800	200	600			
	E	3250	930	2320			
	F	250	—	250			
Total				8170	1296	1250	5624
1%, 100 men	A	5900	2400	3500			
	B	1400	530	870			
	C	3200	1150	2050			
	D	1200	300	900			
	E	3800	1150	2650			
	F	500	100	400			
Total				10,370	1296	2500	6574

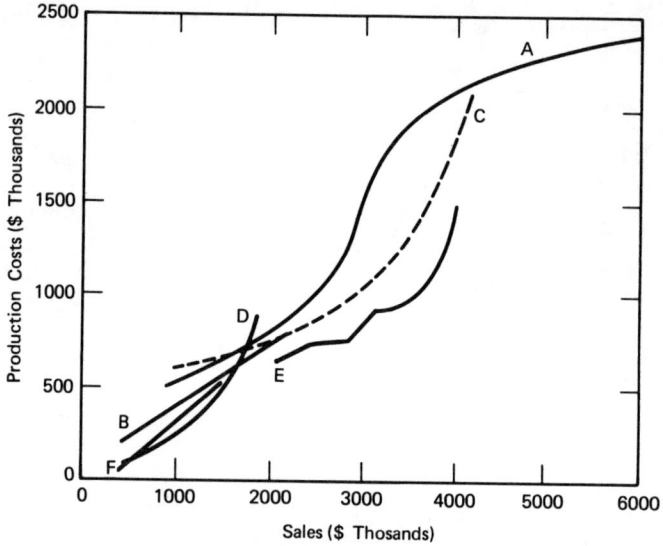

Figure 42   Variable Production Costs

in accordance with overall company objectives. A greatly improved profit picture could be realized by putting on 100 salesmen. The return with only 33 men selling was substantial. Only a 20% increase could be obtained by tripling the sales force. This 20% increase represented $1,136,000, a very tempting goal. Offsetting this was the fact

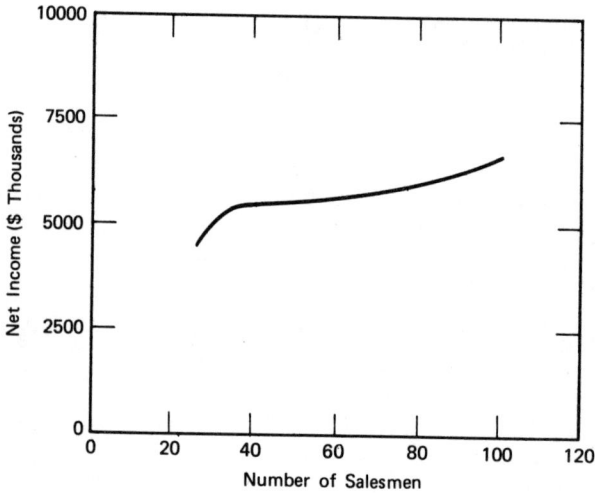

Figure 43   Number of Salesmen versus Income (with Production Costs)

that the estimates for 1971 already represented roughly twice the 1970 actual sales.

Adopting the 100 man sales force would mean the acceptance of the goal of a much greater growth rate than company policy had heretofore desired. The 33-man sales force was more acceptable to management, and, therefore, Di Falco could plan for such an organization. He could use the adjusted table as a control standard for his salesmen. Di Falco noted that the information did not seem to bear out Tolliver's estimate that it might be preferable to push some products over others.

Problem for the Reader

Write a proposal for a profitability concept solution to Di Falco's problem. Indicate the data that is needed and the techniques to be used. Take a guess at whether a new study would support or deny the decision made by management. Other items that you might consider:

1. Devise a production control plan that can optimally react to sales volume variations.
2. Quality control is extremely important to users of automobile parts. What problems can be anticipated for the Peabody Company, relative to the effects of salesmen driven to hard selling to meet difficult goals? How would the quality control system be designed, and what methods could be used to coordinate quality control production to offset ill effects?
3. Determine the percent profit earned by each product in 1970. Using a figure of $100,000 as the desired increase in profit, compute the dollar amount of increase in sales volume to attain this added profit and convert to percent sales increase. Now go through Di Falco's tables and replace his market potential numbers (from his curve) with a number that equals your percent sales increase, increased by unity. For example 40% more in sales are needed to increase profit on Product A by $100,000. Therefore the multiplier equals 1.4. Now recalculate the net return for 1971 for the various territories. Plot the results like Figure 43.

THE WHISTLE TOY COMPANY

The Whistle Toy Company was a conservative firm. It was founded 25 years ago for the purpose of manufacturing a uniquely shaped whistle the success of which led to a series of variations of the basic product. All sold well. The company went on to bigger and better things with a line of games, educational toys, and a number of electrically operated products. These were produced by a substantially supported engineering department.

The company rarely entered the "gimmick" competition (fads and tie-ins to television programs). It was, therefore, growing steadily according to careful and solid plans. The company believed in market research and rarely gambled on new ideas unless the ideas were solidly supported by facts and figures.

Problem for the Reader

You are a junior executive with the Whistle Toy Company, and because you are ambitious, you have prepared a proposal for the production of dolls, a new product for the company. You point out that Curry and Peters make the simplest, most conventional, low priced dolls and are grossing a consistent $1 million per year. Gemco with fad and high-priced, elaborate dolls has reached a peak of $10 million. Gemco profits have not been consistently high, because poor planning has resulted in over-production of the fad dolls.

One can guess that the average net for Gemco was probably less than that of Curry and Peters. These two were not the only ones in the field. The total annual doll market was estimated at close to $100 million and growing at the rate of 10% per year. Competition was keen, but a cursory inspection seemed to show that the biggest business potential was in novelty dolls—talking, walking, and so forth. Electrical and mechanical gadgetry were at the heart of this trade.

Many of the companies producing these dolls spent large sums for research and development in order to be able to compete. Imitators did not do as well as innovators, because they arrived in the market too late to acquire a substantial share of the business peaking at Christmas. To date, no company had, as yet, introduced a successful dancing doll.

Typical engineering and production startup costs for novelty dolls are as high as $500,000. For conventional ones it is as low as $25,000.

You call your project the Go-Go Doll. The Board of Directors has requested that you report on the market research for the doll. There are several questions they will ask. How big is the market? What share of the market can they hope to achieve? Does Whistle Toy have the capability to enter this field? If not, what must they do to develop it? What kind of doll should the company attempt? What is the competition in terms of size, capability, and sales organization? Who are the customers, and what do they want?

You should be able to present an analysis of the market, including analyses of the environment, technical aspects, and the corporate capability. Where data is missing, use your judgment but it would be more advisable to do some research (references: Fortune, Wall St. Journal, Dun and Bradstreet, Standard & Poor's, and Business Week).

Here are some suggestions. A market opportunity matrix can identify the various types of dolls with the customers and the markets. A market opportunity submatrix can supply detailed information about any specific doll; technical, capabilities needed, competition and their capability. The assessment of the company's capability can be presented in a matrix that lists the requirements and availabilities for various elements (engineering, production, etc.) for each type of doll.

Even though you have your heart set on producing the Go-Go doll, do not let this bias show in your analysis. Permit the trade-offs to lead to the correct decisions.

Your intuition has triumphed. With a clear conscience (because of a truly scientific market analysis) you have reported that the Whistle Toy Company should manufacture the Go-Go doll.

The Board has rewarded you with promotion to Program Manager, a tentative title, which will almost certainly be changed to Division Manager, if the program is successful. The Board will not proceed until they approve a detailed program. Their planning manual requires a financial plan for efficient use of the program's budget and an action plan. For the financial plan, the company likes a discounted cash flow analysis of return on their investment. The discounting approach is based on the assumption that the value of money depends not only on its amount but also on the time at which it is available. The computation for this is developed in the following fashion:

The *compound amount* of the original investment at the end of the first year is equal to the original outlay plus the profits; $CA_1 = 1 + r$. At the end of the second year, it is $CA_2 = (CA_1)^2$. At the end of n years, it is $CA_n = (1 + r)^n$. The discounting method is the exact inverse of this compound amount formula. The *discount amount* factor is

$$DA = \frac{1}{(1 + r)^n}$$

where r = rate of return
n = number of time periods (usually years)
CA = compound amount
DA = discount amount

The net discount amount is the sum of the discount amounts for each year. For example, an investment has a return at the end of the first year of $0.24 million and at the end of the second year has earned an additional $720,000. Then

$$NDA = \frac{240,000}{1.2} + \frac{720,000}{1.2 \times 1.2} = \$700,000$$

where $r = 20\%$

You are told to develop your plan for a 5-year period. You have estimated that when the doll is on the market the profits should be $250,000 per year and the reinvestment rate will be 25%. You have a choice of taking one, two, or three years for the engineering and tooling. For each case, the development period gives you a negative return (these are subtracted from the net discount amount) as follows:

One year	$500,000
Two years	150,000 per year
Three years	100,000 per year

Which investment alternative will you choose?

With the finances planned, you can now do a plan for the project. This should cover engineering, design, production, quality control, industrial engineering, marketing, and any other elements you think necessary. You will need to provide action plans for each of these, including budgets, time schedules, and work or task breakdown. Your action plan should determine whether you can live with the proposed budget. Your financial plan should, of course, employ DCR principles.

If the action plan and the financial plan are incompatible, what will you do about it?

CHAPTER 9

IMPLEMENTATION OF DCR PROGRAMS

The preceding chapters were intended to do no more than introduce a new approach to cost reduction. They may have appeared overly long for an introduction, but this was necessary, because a totally new management philosophy must be accepted for success with DCR.

None of the management tools and techniques discussed here are new, although some of the applications may be unusual. The chief difference between static and dynamic cost reduction lies in their objectives. Static cost reduction has for its purpose the solution of a problem. The tools used for static cost reduction are the prescribed instruments for drastic surgery.

DCR is not a panacea. It cannot be substituted for good management. Its purpose is to *maintain* profitability and growth. The tools used for DCR are those necessary to *prevent* problems from occurring.

The requirements for implementing DCR are best defined by comparing the processes of static and dynamic cost reduction.

PREPLANNING

During the preplanning phase, the data needed for developing the company short and long term plans is collected. For SCR, the goals set are usually market share, sales volume and production volume. DCR needs additional goals—profit, cost, and growth. The DCR goals are independent of production capability and productivity. Of course, market forecasts deal with volume in both systems, but, in DCR, the volume is not the primary goal. The DCR volume goal is that volume which can be achieved without impairing profitability and growth.

	SCR	*DCR*
Data collected:	Company policies and objectives. New products. Product improvements. Product pricing. Market forecasts. Productivity.	Company policies and objectives. New products. Product improvements. Product pricing. Profit goals. Growth goals. Cost goals. Profitability. Market forecasts. Customer analysis.
How:	Market research Historical data.	Market research. Historical data. Cost analysis. Sensitivity analysis.
Who:	Marketing. Planning. Production. Engineering.	Marketing. Accounting. Engineering.

PLANNING

	SCR	*DCR*
Output:	Company long term plan. Company short term plan. Budgets. Schedules.	Company long term plan. Company short term plan. Dept. action plans. Contingency plans. Budgets. Schedules.
Who:	Planning Dept.	Planning Committee.

There are three major differences in Planning. One is the DCR department action plans. These are the departmental actions necessary to achieve the objectives of the company plan. Second is the incorporation of contingency plans in all the DCR plans, company or departmental. Lastly, we have the DCR planning committee composed of the managers whose departments are affected by the planning. Included are the departmental financial officers. It is essential for achieving company objectives to have these people involved in the planning.

OPERATIONS

	SCR	*DCR*
Marketing:	Objective is achieving *maximum* sales volume without exceeding marketing budget.	Objective is achieving *optimum* sales volume within profitability goal and cost standards.

	SCR	*DCR*
Production:	Maximum productivity, meeting time and volume schedules.	Meeting time and volume schedules within cost standards.
Other Depts.:	Expedite production and marketing, (i.e. minimization of bottlenecks).	Meet time and volume schedules within cost standards.

Note particularly the establishment of cost standards for *all* departments under DCR.

Let us suppose that a problem occurs, such as reduced profitability, or price cutting by a competitor. Then the following actions would be necessary to solve the problem:

	SCR	*DCR*
Marketing:	Change distribution system. Layoffs. Reduce budget.	Customer analysis. Adjust cost standards. Use contingency plan.
Production:	Layoffs. Industrial engineering. Change manufacturing methods.	Adjust cost standards. Use contingency plan.
Engineering:	Layoffs or increased and speeded-up R&D for product improvement.	No action needed because this department is on the contingency plan always.
Other Depts.:	Layoffs. Procedures analysis.	Adjust cost standards. Use contingency plan.

The benefits of DCR are realized at a time of crisis. DCR can be characterized as preventive medicine for business. For example, note the actions required for the engineering department. In the DCR program, an essential part of the contingency plans is the on going R&D. All the money spent in the engineering department is used for product improvement, new product development, new production techniques and new materials. Any contingency plan must assuredly be built around this R&D.

In the DCR program, because of the sensitivity analysis performed in preplanning, all departments make simultaneous minor adjustments in their cost standards. With SCR, each department makes independent major adjustments.

Sometimes only one department, usually production, will be affected. Note that, with SCR, engineering is rarely synchronized with the future needs of the company. New production techniques are usually developed only after a problem arises.

Product improvement, in most cases, is forced on a company by a more enterprising competitor. New product development is generally a haphazard affair, depending on the creativity of the engineering department. The chief reason for this state of affairs is that engineering is often considered a luxury that only very large companies can afford.

The truth is that few companies can afford to be without engineering support. A DCR program can make engineering affordable by careful planning and budgeting. Without engineering, contingency plans may be ineffective. One should be aware that "engineering" includes data processing personnel. The data processing systems analyst can often obtain economies in systems and procedures that can have an important impact on the profitability.

The importance of engineering is best illustrated by the story of a small electronic instrumentation manufacturer. The company was small but extremely profitable, because it held a number of important patents. Most of its profits were generated by licensing fees. The president decided there was no need to maintain an engineering staff to develop new products or improve the old ones. Current income from licensees was high, and the licensees were making whatever improvements were needed. The entire engineering staff was dismissed. Within two years, the licensees had developed new instruments that were many times superior to the licensor's products.

The basic patents had little value, except as a carrot to induce a major conglomerate to rescue the little company by purchasing it. The conglomerate rebuilt the engineering department.

In summary, DCR is effective, because of better planning, planning that sets interdependent cost standards for all departments. Thus, any required over-all cost adjustment can be achieved by small, simultaneous cost adjustments in all departments. Contingency plans are, therefore, quite simple since they are based on cost sensitivity factors. An important point about DCR is that there need be no major alteration of company procedures, policy, and reporting techniques.

All that is required is a change in management philosophy from a concern for productivity to a concern for profitability.

INDEX

193